JOHN WESLEY

JOHN WESLEY

A Personal Portrait

Ralph Waller

CONTINUUM • NEW YORK

2003

The Continuum International Publishing Group Inc
370 Lexington Avenue, New York, NY 10017

www.continuumbooks.com

First published in Great Britain in 2003 by
SPCK, Holy Trinity Church, Marylebone Road, London NW1 4DU

Library of Congress Cataloging-in-Publication Data

Waller, Ralph.
    John Wesley: a personal history/Ralph Waller.
        p. cm.
Includes bibliographic references and index.
    ISBN 0-8264-1512-1 (pbk.: alk. paper)
1. Wesley, John. 1703–1791. 2. Methodist Church–
    England–Clergy–Biography. 1. Title,
    BX8495.W5.W255 2003
    287'.092–dc21

2003001607

Typeset by Avocet Typeset, Chilton, Aylesbury, Bucks
Printed in Great Britain

Contents

To the memory of

Donald Tranter

Preface

I have written this work for those who know little about John Wesley, or for those who know something about his childhood, his journey to America, and his conversion, and who would like to know more. This book is neither a detailed biography of Wesley, nor is it a systematic treatment of his theology; it is rather a series of studies of major points in Wesley's life and work. Together they reveal a portrait of a person with many failures and disappointments, but they also show a remarkable man endowed with a huge energy, steely determination, and a deep sense of duty to God.

I have tried to resist the double temptation of either hero worship, as found in the works of several of Wesley's earlier biographers, or a desire to cut Wesley down to size, which can be the fate of many great men and women at the hands of modern critics. Wesley was someone whose life was often in a muddle, but this did not obscure his real greatness: his spontaneous generosity, his compassion for his fellow men and women, and his love for his followers and friends, for whom he was their 'father in God'.

I should like to express my grateful thanks to those who have helped me in the writing of this book; first and foremost, Professor Richard Watson of Durham, who kindly read this manuscript and made many helpful suggestions. Without his energetic and scholarly help, this book would have been the poorer. Second, I should like to thank my wife Carol who, although expressing a healthy scepticism for the project from the outset, spent many hours checking references, doing corrections and making useful amendments.

My gratitude is also extended to Elizabeth Machin, my colleague at the Farmington Institute, who typed and retyped this manuscript in an invariably cheerful manner. Joanna Moriarty of SPCK has shown endless patience and great encouragement. My grateful thanks are also due to Dr Williams's Library, the Bodleian Library, and especially to Sue Killoran and Joyce Meakin, the librarians of Harris Manchester College. My deep appreciation goes to John and Cynthia Tudor, who provided books, support and friendship throughout this project.

I must also thank Philip Beuzeval and John Aldridge for reading this manuscript (a lot to ask of friends) and making helpful suggestions. Thanks must also go to the fellows and students of Harris Manchester College and the staff of the Farmington Institute for their patience during the writing of this book, which could so easily have been put aside under the pressure of many other commitments. I am indebted to Rowan Williams and Chris Hughes Smith who preached two of the finest sermons I have ever read on Wesley.

This book is dedicated to the memory of Donald Tranter. It was one of the great joys of life to spend time in his company, conversation and friendship for almost forty years. He himself was a fine Wesley scholar, who represented the very best of Methodism in modern times.

Ralph Waller

The main events in John Wesley's life

1703	17 June	Born at Epworth.
1709	9 February	Saved from the rectory fire.
1714	28 January	Admitted to Charterhouse.
1720	24 June	Enters Christ Church, Oxford.
1726	17 March	Elected Fellow of Lincoln College, Oxford.
1728	22 September	Ordained priest.
1729		Holy Club founded.
1735	25 April	Death of his father.
	21 October	Sails for Georgia.
1738	1 February	Returns to England.
	1 May	Fetter Lane Religious Society founded.
	24 May	John Wesley's conversion.
1739	2 May	First preaches in the open air at Bristol.
1742	30 July	Death of Susanna Wesley.
1744	25 June	First Methodist Conference.
1748	24 June	Opens new Kingswood School.
1751	18 February	Marries Mary Vazeille.
1770	30 September	Death of George Whitefield.
1781	8 October	Death of Mary Wesley.
1784	28 February	Deed of Declaration executed.
	1–2 September	Wesley ordains priests for America and appoints Thomas Coke and Francis Asbury as Superintendents.
1788	29 March	Death of Charles Wesley.
1791	2 March	John Wesley dies at City Road, London.

Chapter 1

Susanna and Samuel

In the summer of 1691, the Reverend Samuel Wesley and his young wife Susanna packed up their books and personal belongings and set out with their son Samuel along the Great North Road from London to begin a new life in Lincolnshire. The journey would not have been an easy one; it would have taken some two to three days. They would have headed northward to Stamford, and then turned eastward to Horncastle and on to the tiny community of South Ormsby nestling in the Lincolnshire Wolds.

Seventeenth-century Lincolnshire has often been portrayed as a backwater of English life.[1] The county was rural, generally poor, and away from the main coaching routes. Its geographical position contributed to its isolation: the North Sea on the east of the county, the wide stretches of the River Humber to the north and the fast-flowing River Trent in the west, with its lowest bridging point at Newark, gave the county a sense of being cut off from the rest of England. But there was also something extraordinary about the place. Perhaps only those who have lived there appreciate the wide skies and flying clouds, the flat, fertile fens in the south, the wolds in the east, and the steep limestone ridge known as the Lincolnshire edge overlooking the Trent valley.

This county, for whatever reason, seemed to attract and produce some great men and women. When Samuel Wesley was presented to the living of South Ormsby on 9 June 1691 by the patrons, Lady Massingberd and her son Burrell Massingberd,[2] Isaac Newton, a Lincolnshire man, was home from Cambridge and working in another rectory at Woolsthorpe, just a few miles to the south on the edge of Grantham. In subsequent years the county was able to boast of John Harrison, the inventor of the nautical chronometer, John Franklin, the explorer, George Boole, the mathematician and author of Boolean Algebra, and Alfred Tennyson, the great Victorian poet. However, two of the greatest of Lincolnshire figures were Samuel Wesley's own sons, John and Charles.

Much has been written in other biographies of Wesley about the difficulties of ministering to the wild and surly people of Lincolnshire. Such a view, though, should be balanced against the many opportunities that the rectorship of South Ormsby offered Samuel, who, with his very light pastoral duties, was able to read and write and foster a love of learning both for himself and for his children. It is also true that his residence in Lincolnshire played a significant part in John's election to a fellowship at Lincoln College, Oxford.

Samuel Wesley's background

Samuel Wesley had been brought up as a Dissenter and came from a long line of Dissenters going back to his grandfather, Bartholomew Wesley, who was born in 1600. Bartholomew's son, John Wesley senior, Samuel's father, had been a minister of the Church of England until he was ejected from office in 1662 for refusing to conform to the Act of Uniformity. He remained in England as a persecuted travelling preacher, but died in 1670 at the age of 34 when his son Samuel was only eight years old. Samuel commenced his formal education at the free school in Dorchester where Henry Dolling was the master. Dolling was a good scholar and had already become well known for his translation into Latin of a widely used Puritan book, *The Whole Duty of Man*.[3] On leaving Dorchester, Samuel Wesley enrolled in Edward Veal's Dissenting Academy at Stepney with a view to entering the Dissenting Ministry. However, he later transferred to the Academy at Newington Green over which Charles Morton presided. Once again Samuel benefited from the guidance of an able scholar. Morton was an energetic man who drew up schemes of logic for his pupils and systematically taught them the arts and sciences. He also set down strict rules for those intending to enter the ministry. He was a republican, however, and on the accession of James II in 1685 Morton, at the age of 58, emigrated to America, where he subsequently became the vice-president of Harvard.

The spiritual pilgrimage from Dissent to the Church of England rectory at South Ormsby had been a long and difficult one for Samuel, and there are at least two different accounts of it. John Wesley's own account is that his father, as one of the most able scholars in the Academy, was given the task of refuting an attack on Dissenters.[4] In the process, Samuel came to the conclusion that the attack was valid, and so turned his back on Dissent and headed for the Church of England.

Samuel's own account of his move is set out in a letter written in 1692 from the vicarage at South Ormsby.[5] In this correspondence he recalls that while he was resident at Mr Morton's Academy he received an income of £40 per year, £10 of which came from Dr Owen and the remaining £30 from Dissenting sources. Dr Owen, a former vice-chancellor of Oxford University, had always harboured the thought that, in a world of constantly changing fortunes, those excluded from matriculation at Oxford through their unwillingness to subscribe to the Thirty-Nine Articles would one day be readmitted to read for degrees. He consequently encouraged students at Dissenting Academies to enter Oxford Colleges without matriculating, and thereby gain the benefits of an Oxford education, although not a degree.

Samuel's time at Oxford

With this encouragement, Samuel Wesley came up to Oxford for a brief experience of university life. Here he found that students and fellows were regularly drunk and often badly behaved, but nevertheless the magic of Oxford made him resolved to return and study in that ancient university. He thus turned his back on Dissent, and walked away from the Dissenting Academy in which he had experienced and learnt so much: to read widely and write fluently, to master Latin and compose poetry, and hear John Bunyan preach on Newington Green. He also left behind the one period of his life when he was comfortably well off on his £40 per year. For the rest of his life Samuel was destined to live in debt, or at least in the shadow of debt.

Samuel Wesley returned to London for three months and made plans to study at Oxford. The opportunity to realize his ambition came through a legacy of several hundred pounds, which had been left to support those intending to become ministers in the Church of England. Twenty pounds was allocated to Wesley, but by the time he had discharged all his debts he had nothing left. This was an experience that would be repeated again and again during his life. However, through the generosity of an elderly friend he was given three pounds, which was sufficient to enrol at Exeter College, and buy a cap and gown. Like students in every age, he had been far too optimistic about his financial affairs and had made no provision to meet the expense of his food and accommodation. Being unable to pay this bill, called 'battels' in Oxford, the fear of being turned out of College loomed large in his mind. Samuel wrote anxious letters to friends and relatives, but no help seemed to be forthcoming.

One morning, in desperation, and with only eight farthings left, he went out early for a walk in the new Oxford parks. As he entered the park he heard a child crying. Under a hedge he found an eight-year-old boy whose clothes had frozen to the ground. He managed to get the small boy to his feet and rubbed his hands and legs to get the circulation going again. On enquiring what had happened, the boy told Samuel that his mother had died some years previously and that three days ago his father had died. He and his ten-year-old sister had waited in the cottage hoping that someone would come, but no one did. They had no food, and no money to buy food, and quickly became weak and hungry. Together they decided that the boy's sister should go to the nearby village and beg, and that he would walk into Oxford to see if he could get food or help. However, having walked such a long way with nothing to eat on a cold morning, he found that he could go no further and so lay down under a hedge in the park.

Samuel put his hand into his pocket and handed over to the boy his last eight farthings, then took him into Oxford to buy bread.[6] When assessing Samuel's character we need to take into account the depth of generosity shown here and balance it against the way he appears to have treated some of his daughters. This story also shows a compassion in Samuel that is not too dissimilar to that later shown by John to the keelmen of Newcastle or the miners of Kingswood. On his return to College, Samuel found that his mother had sent him a large cheese, a relative had left him half a crown, and in the following days his tutor paid his College bills.

Susanna Wesley

Susanna had also made the journey from Dissent to the Church of England, but her starting point was slightly different from that of her husband, Samuel. Her father, Dr Samuel Annesley, had been ordained as a minister in the Church of England in 1644 after graduating from Queen's College, Oxford. In the City of London he had served as Rector of St John's Church in Friday Street and St Giles, Cripplegate, before being ejected from his living in 1662. Because of his wealth he avoided the destitution experienced by many of his fellow displaced clergy and provided financial support for ministers in need. His house in Spital Yard, under the shadow of St Paul's Cathedral, became the centre of a large London network of Dissent.

It was here that Susanna was brought up. She must have witnessed many of the debates around her father's dining table, on Establishment and freedom, on the Prayer Book and the Bible, and on free will and foreknowledge. Among her father's many friends was Richard Baxter, who was a regular visitor to Samuel Annesley's home. Baxter's view of the Catholic Church as an inclusive entity that crossed denominational boundaries helped to shape English Presbyterianism. In her later correspondence with her son, Susanna advocated Baxter's ideas,[7] some of which eventually found expression in John Wesley's sermon of 1749 on 'The Catholic Spirit'. Before Susanna reached the age of 13 she drew up a table listing the main points of controversy between the established Church and Dissent. This exercise brought her to a reasoned judgement as to why she preferred the Church of England.[8]

Susanna met Samuel Wesley in 1682, at her sister Elizabeth's wedding to John Dunton, the publisher.[9] Five years later, after Samuel had graduated from Oxford, they were married, on 12 November 1688. It is easy to see why he was attracted to her. Susanna was young and beautiful and came from a cultured and learned family with aristocratic roots. Her grandfather had been a peer of the realm, and her great-uncle was the Earl of Anglesey. To Samuel, coming from his relatively poor and lowly background, the prospect of marrying into a large family with wealth and principles must have been very appealing. To Susanna, the young Samuel, recently graduated from Oxford, bright, clever, and sharing her principles, must have seemed equally captivating. He was shortly to be ordained priest. So began a marriage that was to last 46 years.

Samuel as Rector of South Ormsby

After three short appointments within the Church of England, two of which were curacies in London and the other a naval chaplaincy, Samuel Wesley was appointed Rector of South Ormsby in 1691. The Lincolnshire rectory to which they came is described on several occasions as 'a mean cot'. This description comes from one of Samuel's poems written at the time:

> In a mean cot, composed of reeds and clay,
> Wasting in sighs th' uncomfortable day;
> Near where the inhospitable Humber roars,
> Devouring by degrees the neighbouring shores,
> Let earth go where it will I'll not repine,
> Nor can unhappy be, while heaven is mine.[10]

However, the house was an altogether more substantial affair than this suggests, according to the description made by his successor: 'Consisting of four Bays of Building, the kitchen now annexed to the House, one Barn, one stable, a Garden and Orchard.'[11] It was in this house that Samuel wrote some of his best works and also found time to write poetry about his young wife:

> She graced my humble roof, and blest my life,
> Blest me by a far greater name than wife; . . .[12]

One son, Samuel, had been born before they arrived in South Ormsby. The parish records show that a daughter, Susanna, was baptized in March 1692, and another, Emily, was baptized in January 1693. The baby Susanna died at the end of her first year, and two infant boys, Annesley and Jehidiah, were buried in January 1695.[13] In spite of the infant mortality, so common at the time, Samuel and Susanna found it increasingly difficult to manage financially with a growing family. Samuel had no wealthy relatives who could help him and so he had to look for financial help from a patron, or from writing, or from taking on an additional curacy. In fact, he tried all three. The Marquis of Normanby, his patron, continued to help him and in 1694 even recommended him to Archbishop Tillotson as a candidate for the vacant Irish bishopric of Ross and Cloyne.[14] Sadly for Samuel, King William, when consulted, seemed less than enthusiastic. However, it was Samuel's own writing that eventually appeared to provide a way to a more substantial living. Shortly before Queen Mary died in 1694, Samuel dedicated his poem in ten books, *The Life of Our Blessed Lord and Saviour Jesus Christ*, to her. He was rewarded with the living of Epworth, in north-west Lincolnshire, to which he was appointed in 1695 (although the Wesleys did not take up residence until two years later), and where John (1703) and Charles (1707) were born.

Chapter 2

Epworth and the Rectory

John Wesley was born on 17 June 1703 into a large family living in the rectory at Epworth. Four things dominated the family during his childhood: debt, the rectory fire, education, and the tempestuous relationship of his parents. In a letter to the Society for Promoting Christian Knowledge (SPCK), written in 1701, Samuel Wesley described Epworth in some detail. It had a population of 1,100 people and was the chief town of the marshy 'Island of Axholme', which had a total population of some 7,000 people. He noted that there was no public school for the children of the area and suggested that it would be of great benefit if a charity school could be founded in the town. Less than one in twenty of the population could recite the Lord's Prayer, and perhaps only one in thirty could recite the Creed.

Samuel had made it his business to teach the population. Those who could afford to pay gave £10 per year, which went towards the salary of an assistant teacher. There were no Roman Catholics or Presbyterians in the parish, but there were about forty Quakers and approximately seventy Anabaptists, who insulted him wherever he went. He estimated that there were approximately one hundred people living in Epworth who had little or no religion at all. He also stated that he had set up monthly services of Holy Communion, but that no more than twenty people were ever in attendance. Hardly anyone in the parish would assist him, and for this reason he pleaded that he urgently required the prayers, advice and continued correspondence of the SPCK. He told the Society that he was not without hope – indeed, he had great expectations from a local SPCK branch that he had established, consisting of ten to twelve clergymen. The letter also mentioned that many of the poor people of the parish wanted Bibles and other books, but he was unable to supply them, although in the past he had often bought books with his own money and given them to those in need.

A second letter written by Samuel Wesley to the Secretary of the SPCK at about the same time expressed his gratitude to the Society for its timely help in sending him lists of books and inviting him to select free of charge any titles he might wish to have. He took full advantage of this kind offer, and among the many publications he selected were: 'Acc^s of Charity Schools, D. Woodward's Sermons on the same subject, Forms of Subscription, Orders of Schools, Dr. W.'s Acc^s of Religious Societies, Account of the Workhouses at Bristol, Accounts of the French Protestants sufferings in the Gallies, History of the Societies for Reformation, Help to a National Reformation, Vindication of Informers, Caution to Profane Swearers (although he added that there were but a few in his parish) and Persuasive to the Observing the Lord's Day'; the last, he maintained, was 'extremely wanted among them'.[1]

From these two letters we have a graphic insight not only into the state of the parish in the opening years of the eighteenth century, but also into the Rector's isolation and his efforts to improve the religious life of those in the region.

Samuel's description of his attempt to set up a local branch of the SPCK is also significant, and John undoubtedly learned something from his father's efforts when he came to form the United Societies.[2] It is also of interest to note that much of the reading matter that Samuel Wesley requested was concerned with education, religious societies, care for the poor, and the development of the spiritual life – all causes to which John Wesley later devoted his energies.

Samuel and debt

Henry Rack reminds us[3] that Samuel Wesley had many good qualities: he was learned, zealous and pious, and could be affectionate. He was also a very brave man, but with his courage went an obstinacy and a narrow-mindedness. Whatever his good and bad points might have been, on one thing nearly all his critics and supporters are agreed: he was a poor manager of money. Because of this naïvety in regard to home economics, a large black cloud of debt hung over the rectory at Epworth for most of his incumbency.

Samuel Wesley's financial problems had begun long before he came to Epworth. In a long letter of 30 December 1700[4] written to Dr John Sharp, the Archbishop of York, Samuel set out the details of his own financial history. He confessed that he was ashamed of being £300 in debt when he had an annual stipend of £200. He pointed out that for seven years prior to coming to Epworth he had an income of only £50 per year, and through various circumstances he had fallen into debt to the tune of £150.[5] However, the greatest problem he faced was that his family kept on increasing: three additional children had been born in the three years he had been at Epworth, and three more surviving children would be added to the family total in the years that followed.[6]

The Archbishop did raise the sum of almost £185, for which Samuel was most grateful, but it still did not get him to the position he desired: of clearing all his debts and not being 'called upon for money' before he had made it.[7] Worse was to come, for in May 1705 there was a contested election in Lincolnshire. When Samuel supported the opposition to a certain Colonel Whichcott, Whichcott's friends demanded immediate repayment of a small loan of some £30. Being unable to repay the whole sum, Samuel was arrested as a debtor and imprisoned in Lincoln Castle.

Two observations come out of this sad episode: the heroic nature of Samuel when faced with the difficulties of prison,[8] and the humiliation of a family who were immersed in debt. Samuel not only stoically endured prison, but in this new setting continued to perform his priestly duties, as his letter to Archbishop Sharp indicates:

> Lincoln Castle, June 25th 1705
>
> I don't despair of doing some good here . . . and it may be, do more in this new parish than in my old one; for I have leave to read prayers every morning and afternoon here in the prison, and to preach once a Sunday, which I choose to do in the afternoon, when there is no sermon at the Minster. And I am getting acquainted with my brother jail-birds as fast as I can; and shall write to London next post, to the Society for Propagating Christian Knowledge, who, I hope, will send me some books to distribute among them.[9]

On 7 September he reported that Susanna had sent him her rings so that he could sell them and then get better treatment in prison. Here again he showed great dignity in returning them immediately. Samuel remained uncomplainingly in prison for three months, while friends and supporters raised sufficient funds to have him released. Meanwhile Susanna, who was having a difficult time at home, corresponded with Archbishop Sharp. In reply to his enquiry as to whether the family had ever gone without food, she penned a few lines that many who have been in debt would be able to identify with:

> My Lord,
> . . . I will freely own to your grace, that strictly speaking, I never did want bread. But then I have had so much care to get it before 'twas eat, and to pay for it after, as has often made it very unpleasant to me. And I think to have bread on such terms is the next degree of wretchedness to having none at all.[10]

Samuel's release from prison in 1705, and his taking on the additional parish of Wroot, did not end his financial problems. In 1721 Susanna wrote a long, begging letter to her brother Samuel Annesley, but it brought little reward to the family. It is interesting that John Wesley, who grew up in an atmosphere of pervasive debt, spent so much of his time and energy in later life feeding, clothing and educating poor people, and providing shelter for them. Stories of his father's imprisonment may also have been one reason why, at Oxford, he and his friends took such an interest in visiting and comforting the prisoners in the city gaol.

The rectory fire

The great fire at the Epworth Rectory has become a central part of the Methodist story. It has been painted, preached on, written about, and thought of as one of the great building blocks of Methodism. At the heart of the incident was the deliverance, when all hope was lost, of a small child from an upper window of the blazing rectory. This episode came to be seen by his mother, and by later generations of Methodists, as a special deliverance by God so that the child could undertake some great work for God in the future.

The fire of 1709 was not the first to damage the rectory, for three-quarters of it had been destroyed by a fire in broad daylight in 1702. On that occasion, as with the great fire of 1709, Samuel was philosophical. He wrote to Archbishop Sharp:

> My wife, children and books were saved . . . I shall go on, by God's assistance, to take my tithe; and when that is in, to rebuild my house, having at last crowded my family into what's left, and not missing many of my goods.[11]

In a series of letters to her son Samuel and to the Reverend Joseph Hoole, Susanna Wesley gave a detailed account of the 1709 fire which completely destroyed the rectory. The fire was discovered between 11 o'clock and midnight when all the members of the family were in bed. They made rapid moves to evacuate the rectory, and did not even have time to get dressed. From this account Samuel appears to have been something of a hero; he broke open the nursery door and instructed the maid to bring down the children. Even though surrounded by flames, he raced upstairs to get the keys to the house only moments before the staircase caught fire. When the street door was opened and the flames roared in, he had the presence of mind to lead his household to the garden door. He carried the children into the garden, from where he heard a cry for help from the nursery; several times Samuel attempted to climb the stairs, but found that it was impossible to get near to the young John. It was only then that he knelt down and commended the boy's soul to God. At this point in the story John himself deserves some credit, because, not being able to get down the stairs because of the flames, and at the moment when his bed caught fire, he climbed up to the casement window, where he was seen by a man in the courtyard below, who immediately clambered up to the window and pulled him out at the very last moment before the burning roof fell in: 'So by the infinite mercy of almighty God our lives were well preserved by little less than [a] miracle, for there passed but a few moments between the first discovery of the fire and the falling of the house.'[12]

The climax of the events of the fateful night reveals both a deep sense of devotion to God expressed in thanksgiving, combined with an ability to discern the truly valuable things of life. Susanna described the scene in her letter of 24 August 1709: the family members, with no clothes on, stood in the yard of the rectory; the house was destroyed and with it their money, food, clothing and possessions; the children were crying because of the fear of the fire and the piercing frost attacking their bare feet; and yet the parents' minds were filled with a sense of the goodness of God in preserving their and their children's lives.[13]

Samuel Wesley, as ever impatient, immediately started rebuilding the rectory and completed the task in less than a year. Although it appeared that he had collected sufficient funds to pay for the construction, some 13 years later, in 1722, the house was still only half furnished, and the money he had borrowed to replace the furniture and buy new clothes had still not been repaid.[14]

Educating the Wesley children

Whether this fire was deliberately started by Samuel's enemies or whether it was just bad luck we shall never know. However, the Epworth Rectory fire became an icon of Methodism, and was to be a point of reference in John Wesley's interpretation of his own life. Likewise, one of the consequences of the fire for Susanna was to cause a partial renaissance in her life. God had delivered her children, so she must now re-double her efforts to provide a first-class education for them. This resolution was also coupled with the desire to develop her own religious life.[15] For John Wesley, the fire became a milestone, to which he referred at various stages in his life. Perhaps under his mother's influence it caused him to see himself as 'a brand plucked from the burning'.[16] These were not only the words that formed the motto of his Journals,[17] but also the inscription under Henry Parker's picture of the Epworth Rectory engulfed in flames, which in a subsequent century found a place in so many Methodist homes, schoolrooms and vestries.

Susanna Wesley has been looked upon as a great educationalist among Methodist people for the way in which she brought up and taught her large family. In 1732 John Wesley asked her to write down the educational methods that she used, and this she did in a letter to him later that year. After her death, he published the letter in his Journal and in the *Arminian Magazine*. Running through her educational principles there was a strong note of control, not only in terms of formal learning, but also in the area of behaviour. Corporal punishment, never eating between meals, and eating what was provided at mealtimes were all part of Susanna's regime.[18] Her major aim was to get children away from what she called 'self will' into a disciplined life where duty to God and to others was paramount. No child was ever given what he or she 'cried' for, but the children were taught to ask politely for what they wanted.[19]

Susanna's children had to learn the Lord's Prayer as soon as they could speak, and even before they could talk they were instructed in distinguishing between the Sabbath Day and other days of the week. None of the children, except the youngest, was ever taught to read until he or she was five years old. Susanna also set out various rules that supported her educational practice. No child accused of some misdemeanour should ever be beaten if he or she owned up and promised to mend his or her ways. Every act of obedience should be commended and rewarded. Promises had to be strictly kept, and a gift – once bestowed – belonged to the person to whom it was given. No act of lying, or stealing, or indeed playing in church, should go unpunished.

From a twenty-first-century perspective Susanna's system of education does not seem very revolutionary; much of it, in fact, was drawn from Puritan tradition. Not all the recipients of the programme flourished in later life, though; the girls were particularly badly affected. However, for John Wesley it laid a foundation of discipline, honesty, hard work and the constructive use of time, which became the basic structure of his adult life. There is also a resemblance between the rules laid down by Susanna and the rules that John Wesley later set out for his preachers and for members of his Societies.[20]

Friction between Samuel and Susanna

The rectory at Epworth had much to offer to the children growing up there in terms of environment: a good sound education, access to books, and the good moral example of their parents. One thing it did not offer, though, was a calm domestic life, owing to the tempestuous relationship between Samuel and Susanna. In a letter to John, written in 1725 while he was considering ordination, Susanna confessed, 'But 'tis an unhappiness almost peculiar to our family, that your father and I seldom think alike.'[21] On this occasion Susanna was in support of John being ordained as a priest in the Church of England, while his father appeared to be less certain.

Another illustration of their stormy relationship occurred in the winter of 1711–12 when Samuel was at the meeting of Convocation in London and he received news from an acting curate that Susanna was conducting services in the rectory in his absence. There appears to be more behind his rebuke to her than simply church order. It would not be surprising if an element of jealousy had crept into his reprimand, as Susanna's services in the rectory were apparently proving more popular than the worship conducted by her husband or his temporary curate in the parish church.

The turbulence of the marriage across the years was not only felt by Samuel and Susanna, but was also recognized by their children. Samuel Junior, in a letter written to his brother John in 1727, expressed a heartfelt wish that their parents could be more in harmony with each other.[22] John Wesley himself was well aware of the friction between his parents and once wrote, 'Were I to write my own life, I should begin it before I was born, merely for the purpose of mentioning a disagreement between my father and my mother.'[23]

The incident he was referring to occurred one morning when Susanna omitted to say 'Amen' at family prayers when Samuel had prayed for King William III. On his enquiring as to the reason for this omission, Susanna replied, 'Because I do not believe the Prince of Orange to be King.'[24] Her view, held by many 'non-jurors', was that James II was still the rightful King of England. The issue for Susanna was not that of James or William, but of the liberty of conscience. This had been a strong principle in the nonconformity of her father's house. Samuel flew into a rage and informed his wife that if she held this view they must part. He shouted the now famous lines, 'if we have two kings we must have two beds'.[25] He went to his study and shortly afterwards set out for London, where he remained at Convocation for the rest of the year.

In John Wesley's own account of this event it appears that Samuel remained in London until 8 March 1702, when, on the death of King William, the Rector and his wife agreed that the new Queen Anne was the legitimate monarch of England. However, it appears from Susanna's correspondence with Lady Yarborough that the issue was more protracted than John Wesley believed. It seems that on her refusal to say 'Amen', Samuel 'immediately kneeled down and imprecated the divine Vengeance upon himself and all his posterity if ever he touched me more or came into a bed with me before I had begged God's pardon and his for not saying Amen to the prayer for the Kg'.[26] From the correspondence it is clear that Susanna felt that she would be mocking God by begging pardon for something that she did not consider to be a sin. It is also clear that Samuel was equally stubborn, and even after the death of King William he was seeking a naval chaplaincy on a warship.

For six months the marriage was disrupted by this political quarrel, but duty as ever won the day with Samuel, for when he received news of the first fire at Epworth Rectory, on the last day of July 1702, he put aside his vow and galloped home as quickly as he could to take care of his wife and family in their moment of need. The child of their reconciliation, John Wesley, was born the following June.

Chapter 3

Charterhouse and Christ Church

When John Wesley was ten, in January 1714, he secured a place at Charterhouse School in London through the good offices of the Duke of Buckingham, a family friend. Thomas Sutton had founded the school in 1611, for the education of poor children. A few years before Wesley arrived, Joseph Addison, the poet and essayist, had been a pupil there, as had Bishop Martin Benson of Gloucester (1689–1752).

The effect of Charterhouse on John Wesley

Public schools in the eighteenth century could be hostile environments for young children, who were often bullied and forced to undertake a constant round of duties and tasks for the older boys. Many of these unkind practices continued until the great reforms introduced in the nineteenth century by Thomas Arnold at Rugby and Godfrey Thring at Uppingham. It appears that Wesley did not suffer too much from physical abuse but, like all the other boys, he found that much of his food was taken by the older ones. Looking back on this period of his life almost sixty years later, he was able to see he had benefited greatly from this practice:

> I can hardly believe that I am this day entered into the sixty-eighth year of my age. How marvellous are the ways of God. How has he kept me even from a child. From ten to thirteen or fourteen I had little but bread to eat, and not great plenty of that. I believe this was so far from hurting me, that it laid the foundation of lasting health.[1]

Wesley came to believe that another practice he adopted at Charterhouse also assisted in his good health: at the suggestion of his father he ran round the school grounds three times every morning. Throughout this period there is also evidence that he worked hard at his lessons. His older brother, Samuel, who was also in London at this time as an Usher at Westminster School, wrote to their father, 'Jack is with me, and a brave boy learning Hebrew as fast as he can.'[2] John also developed a great liking for Latin verse, which he continued to compose at Oxford.[3]

Looking back at his time at Charterhouse, Wesley felt that he had neglected some of the outward duties of religion and was also continuously guilty of committing outward sins.[4] Tyerman has interpreted Wesley's confession in such a way as to suggest that Wesley left home as a saint and returned from school as a sinner. But there is evidence that he continued to read his Bible, say his prayers, and go to church. Indeed, it is not surprising that he had a rebellion when away from the strict regime of Epworth. It would have been part of the normal process of growing up. His schooldays seem not to have been a particularly unhappy period of his life, for he was delighted a few years later to return to Charterhouse in 1727 and act as steward on the School Founder's Day in December. In later years he would go out of his way to walk through the school grounds at least once a year.

In one particular respect Charterhouse served him well, for the school was fortunate to have several scholarships to Oxford and Cambridge Colleges. John Wesley was privileged to be awarded one of these scholarships from Charterhouse: an Exhibition to Christ Church, Oxford, with a stipend of £20 per year to be paid in quarterly instalments. It was due to a confusion as to whether he had received this allowance twice in one term as an undergraduate at Christ Church that we have his earliest recorded letter, written to the treasurer of Charterhouse, Mr Ambrose Eyre. He apologized to the treasurer for the error and thanked him for putting 'the most favourable construction' on the transaction.[5]

His time at Christ Church

Wesley entered Christ Church in 1720, although we know very little about his time as an undergraduate. The main evidence is in three surviving letters from John to his mother for the period 1720–4. From these letters, together with two replies from her, we can catch a few glimpses of his life at Oxford. In a letter dated 23 September 1723 he informed his mother that he had changed his tutor as a result of the retirement of the Reverend George Wigan. Wesley was fortunate to have been taught by Wigan, who was looked upon as 'a great and very good tutor',[6] with expertise in both Hebrew and the English language. Wigan resigned from his tutorial duties to concentrate on his responsibilities of being Rector to the Parish of Old Swinford in Worcestershire, where he died in office in 1776.[7]

The Reverend Henry Sherman, who replaced Wigan, took a kindly interest in Wesley and his brother Charles, an interest that went beyond his strict tutorial duties. On one occasion he breakfasted with John[8] and on another he accompanied him to inspect the rooms that had been assigned to Charles.[9] He also brought to John news of the Wesley family, and after John graduated Sherman gave him several books that he believed would be useful to him.[10]

From these letters we also learn that John's brother Samuel was very helpful to him while he was an undergraduate. John managed financially as a result of help from his brother Samuel, and the Exhibition from Charterhouse.[11]

His health was also good. While he was at Oxford there was an outbreak of smallpox which, John reported to his mother, had already claimed the life of one undergraduate at Christ Church. John himself, although unaffected by this disease, suffered from a severe nose bleed, which in the end he managed to stop by jumping into a cold river.[12] It is an indication of the closeness of the Wesley family that he always wished to be remembered to his sisters and made it clear he would be pleased to receive letters from any of them.

In later letters he tells of a gentleman undergraduate at Christ Church whose cap and wig were stolen as he stood at the door of a coffee house at seven o'clock one evening. John reassured his mother that this could not happen to him as he wore neither. Indeed, in those days, and for the rest of his life, he wore his hair long in order to save money on haircuts.[13] His letters refer also to national events such as the sensational escape of Jack Sheppard, a condemned prisoner, from the cells of Newgate Prison, and the equally interesting escape of Brigadier William Mackintosh who served in the army of the Old Pretender and took part in the Jacobite Rebellion of 1714.

The correspondence also shows John's keen interest in supernatural events, and he recounted in detail two such events that he had heard of. The first concerned the aged Bishop of Raphoe, who had in his diocese a young man boasting that he was constantly being lifted up into the air by invisible hands and taken to a great feast. The young man said he was threatened with the penalty of death by members of the festive party if he told anyone of his experiences. One day the Bishop persuaded him to tell the full story, with the consequence that soon after this the man died. A prophecy the young man had made shortly before his death was also fulfilled, in that the Bishop never moved into his newly constructed palace as it appeared to be haunted. Wesley made no comment on the story except to attribute the evil to the Devil, but it is curious that he should have spent time on it: it is early evidence of his lifelong interest in the supernatural. He also related to his mother the episode concerning three Christ Church students who late one evening were crossing the fields when a white translucent figure appeared in front of them. It was discovered later that the mother of one of the young men had died at exactly the same time as the figure was seen.

Apart from the supernatural, another subject that interested him was health, especially his own. In a letter to his mother on 1 November 1724, he drew attention to Dr Cheyne's book called *Health and Long Life*. Cheyne's essential theory was that good health and long life depended on temperance in eating and drinking, combined with plenty of exercise. He was against eating highly salted food and recommended drinking two pints of water and one pint of wine every 24 hours. Cheyne also advocated eating only a small amount of meat and a slightly larger amount of vegetables each day. Wesley became a follower of Cheyne's regime, and at the age of 68, when he was still amazingly active, Wesley wrote in his Journal, 'in consequence of reading Dr Cheyne, I chose to eat sparingly and drink water. This was another great means of continuing my health . . .'[14]

In 1724 John Wesley graduated with a BA degree from Oxford, but stayed on in his rooms at Christ Church to prepare for his MA. At the age of 21, as a graduate of the university, he was ready to commence the next stage of his life as an Oxford academic.

Chapter 4

Lincoln College and a Fellow's Life

The year 1726 was an important one for John Wesley, for in the September of the previous year it had become known to the Wesley family that a fellowship would become vacant at Lincoln College, Oxford, through the forthcoming resignation of a Mr Thorald. This fellowship was of particular interest as it was traditionally held by a Lincolnshire man. Samuel Wesley, who like many graduates saw Oxford through rose-coloured spectacles, was greatly attracted by the idea that one of his sons should become a Fellow of an Oxford college. He immediately started lobbying on behalf of John, contacting the Rector (Head of College) of Lincoln, Dr Morley, who also held the nearby Lincolnshire living of Scotton. Samuel also canvassed the Bishop of Lincoln, who was the College Visitor, and Sir John Thorald, whose son was vacating the fellowship.[1] John's elder brother, Samuel, also did his best to prepare him for the appointment. Understandably, there was great family rejoicing when John was elected to the position on 17 March 1726.[2]

A fellowship at Lincoln College

To be a Fellow of Lincoln College was of great importance to John Wesley. First, it brought him parental approval, and the letters he wrote to his parents over the years provide a clear indication of his desire to seek their advice and have their support. Second, his election enabled him to remain in Oxford: from his student days onwards the magnetism of Oxford had attracted him – so much so that he was unable to break away from it until he was well into middle age. The fellowship also meant that not only could he remain in close contact with Oxford, but he could also now feel that he belonged – not only to the university, but also to a group of very pleasant and welcoming Fellows. He wrote:

> As far as I have ever observed, I never knew a college besides ours, whereof the members were so perfectly satisfied with one another and so inoffensive to the other part of the University. All I have yet seen of the Fellows

are both well-natured and well-bred; men admirably disposed as well to preserve peace and good neighbourhood among themselves, as to promote it wherever else they have any acquaintance.[3]

There is evidence that Wesley himself was warmly received by the other Fellows of the College,[4] and we must also not forget the religious appeal of Oxford to John Wesley. Alongside all the criticism of religion being in decline in the eighteenth century, there were devout men and women in Oxford, and there was a quality of worship in Christ Church Cathedral, St Mary's University Church, the College chapels, and even the city churches, that would have greatly appealed to him.

Wesley's fellowship at Lincoln also put him in a position where he no longer had to worry about his finances. At first his stipend was not sufficient to give him total financial security: indeed in November he received an account from the Bursar showing that he was in debt to the College for a sum in excess of £3.[5] This was largely due to the fact that he was not resident and was having to pay his entry fee to the Senior Common Room and his share of the Senior Common Room expenses. But once he took up residence this situation soon changed, and his fellowship also enabled him to earn additional money by tutoring students, taking on curacies, and through writing and preaching.

One of the delightful periods in taking up any new post is the time between being appointed and actually taking up the responsibilities of the appointment. John Wesley extended this period by writing to the Rector of Lincoln College to seek permission to be out of residence from April to September 1726. He thus spent Easter in Oxford and then set out to walk to Epworth. He had always enjoyed walking, and in old age attributed his good health to this exercise, but this particular journey was undertaken on foot more as a result of a lack of money than for health or recreational reasons.

A summer idyll: 1726

For John Wesley, the summer of 1726 was one of those long, happy and idyllic times that come very rarely. Susanna, his mother, was pleased to show off her new Oxford academic, and John accompanied her on various visits. Some of his sisters were now married: Sukey to a local farmer, Anne to a local land agent and surveyor, and Hetty to a plumber. The other four sisters were still at home, and he read to them in the long summer evenings. He also worked in the garden, making an arbour with benches. He visited friends in the neighbourhood at Loughton and Bawtry, Doncaster, Gainsborough and Owston Ferry, and preached at nearby churches. He swam in the river, probably the Trent or Vermuyden's drainage channels. He worked in the fields and made hay with his sisters, and picked the fruit and collected the flowers. He took up the duties of a curate at Wroot, helping his father. He indulged his interest in the supernatural and devoted several hours to assembling accounts of unexplained disturbances in the rectory at Epworth. On 12 September he crossed the Trent and visited the Head of his College in his parish at Scotton. Throughout the summer he read a great deal: sometimes light reading, including several Restoration plays, and sometimes solid theological works taken from the Rector's library.

One of his pleasant companions of that happy summer was Kitty Hargreaves. Naturally enough, Wesley as a young man found it hard to resist emotional entanglements with clever, attractive young women. In later life he laid down some severe rules for his followers about not being alone with young women, and these rules probably grew out of his own experiences. Kitty Hargreaves and John Wesley spent much time together that summer, as can be seen through the constant mention of her name in his diary of this time. The visits she made to the rectory became so frequent that on one occasion Samuel Wesley sent her away on the grounds that she was 'courting' John.

Reading between the lines it seems as if there was more to this relationship than just two friends of the opposite sex walking, talking and reading together. John Wesley was falling in love with Kitty Hargreaves and, as so often happened with his relationships with women, he could not decide whether he wanted to or not. On one occasion he wrote, 'Never touch Kitty's hand again', but continued to see her. By 13 August he seems to have gone further than touching Kitty's hand for he resolved that he would never touch a woman's breasts again. Even with his return to Oxford, Kitty does not fade from the scene. Three years later he visited her in Gainsborough and met her in Burford in the summer of 1730 for a very enjoyable tea 'and rhymes'. Later, in 1732, he stopped off in Lincoln to visit his sister Kezzy, who by now was a pupil teacher at Mrs Taylor's school. It seems likely that he also saw Kitty on this occasion, for she was probably a fellow teacher at the school.[6]

The major serious work he had accomplished that summer was writing numerous sermons, helping his father complete his book on Job, and writing his paraphrase on Psalm 104.

One incident marred this long, happy summer. Samuel Wesley was a harsh disciplinarian when he felt that a point of principle had been breached. His daughter Hetty had always been something of a free spirit, rebelling against the austere regime of the Epworth Rectory. She fell in love with a young lawyer, Will Attkins. When it was discovered that she had spent a night away from home with him, the relationship was terminated. Hetty was then married off to a rough and uncouth plumber, William Wright, who was often drunk. Hetty was condemned to a squalid life of misery, unhappiness and isolation, as her father refused ever to speak to her or have her in the home again.

Most members of the Wesley family sided with Samuel over this, but John, who had a deep sense of compassion for those in trouble and a concern for his sister, wanted to change his father's view. Having been assured by his father that it was his duty to point out to others the faults he saw in them, he proceeded to preach a sermon at Wroot on 28 August on the theme of love that knows no limits. The sermon was entitled 'Universal Charity – or the charity due to wicked persons'. It was some days later, while out for a walk with his brother Charles, that John learnt that the sermon had upset his father. He returned home immediately to apologize and make peace. Both men shed tears, and the relationship between them was restored[7] – but sadly not that between Hetty and her father. Shortly after this incident, on 21 September, John returned to Oxford.

His return to Oxford

Oxford Colleges are governed by the Head of the College and Fellows, most of whom are academics and teachers. In 1726 Lincoln College had 12 Fellows and a rector, Dr Morley, who as Head of the College had one vote, the same as each Fellow, and a casting vote in the event of a tie. By and large, Oxford Colleges were governed by consensus, and the Rector of the College would exercise a supervision over the College by personality rather than by power. In the event of a major disagreement between members of the Governing Body, which could not be settled by a vote, the Visitor of the College, the Bishop of Lincoln, would be called upon to decide the issue.

Lincoln College in the first half of the eighteenth century seemed to be a happy home for John Wesley, and remarkably free of division. It was a good place to study and provided a new academic stimulus for him. He wrote about the move from Christ Church:

> Removing to another [Lincoln] College I began to see more and more the value of time. I applied myself closer to study. I watched more carefully against actual sins. I advised others to be religious, according to that scheme of religion by which I modelled my own life.[8]

Within a few months of returning to Oxford he wrote to his mother to tell her that he was preparing for his MA degree and setting out a scheme of systematic study. He also pointed out that because life was short, and time valuable, he was being very selective about what he read.[9]

For the remaining weeks of the autumn of 1726, and through the winter months, he worked on his MA alongside his many other activities. He took the degree on 14 February, delivering the three required lectures in Latin. The subjects were the souls of animals, Julius Caesar, and the love of God. Tyerman makes the point that these disputations afforded him a considerable reputation.[10] His general reading at this time was extensive and he developed two skills that helped him to study. While on a journey to Epworth, he and Charles discovered that they could walk and read at the same time.[11] This realization not only fitted in with his new desire not to waste time, but also enabled him to increase greatly the number of books he read. Second, he developed the habit of reading every book twice.[12] On the first reading he would skim quickly through a book so that he had a good idea of its contents; on the second reading he would make notes and copy out important passages.

Wesley's plan for studying

Wesley's plan of study for 1727 makes interesting reading: Monday and Tuesday were given over to the Classics; Wednesday to ethics and logic; Thursday was devoted to the ancient languages of Hebrew and Arabic; Friday to philosophy and metaphysics; Saturday to poetry and rhetoric; Sunday to the study of theology.[13] He permitted himself to study on Sundays, but limited this to theology. He often preached on a Sunday in the villages surrounding Oxford – sometimes in two places on the same day.

Wesley wrote to his brother Samuel on 5 December 1726: 'Leisure and I have taken leave of one another.' Under this regime of study he rapidly devoured books. In theology, for example, his reading covered a wide range of interests and opinions, not only the Early Church Fathers whose writings he considered to be second only to the Bible, but also the Reformation and modern theology. He read Justin Martyr, *First Apology*, St Augustine, *Confessions*, St Bernard, *Meditations*, John Pearson, *Exposition of the Creed*, and William Wake, *Apostolic Epistles*. His general reading was wide-ranging, including for example reading Halley, *On Magnetism and Gravity*, in 1725, and in 1729 he read Voltaire, *Essay on the French Civil Wars*. V. H. H. Green in Appendix I of his *Young Mr Wesley* sets out a very useful list of the books and plays that Wesley read in the nine years between 1725 and 1734, totalling some 580 known works. Three books, in particular, had a profound effect on his developing Christian faith; they were Jeremy Taylor, *Holy Living and Holy Dying*, Thomas à Kempis, *The Imitation of Christ*, and the newly published (1728) William Law, *A Serious Call to a Devout and Holy Life*. There is a strong suggestion that Wesley was encouraged to read Jeremy Taylor and Thomas à Kempis by Sarah Kirkham, the sister of a close friend, Robert Kirkham. These books began to make a significant impact upon him towards the end of 1725. Indeed, when he came to write his own *Plain Account of Christian Perfection* (1765), he recorded the importance of his readings of Taylor, à Kempis and Law.

His letters to his mother written in 1725 clearly show that by this time he was familiar with both Thomas à Kempis and Jeremy Taylor. In a letter of 18 June he expressed some sympathy with Taylor's view that the Christian life must be lived in humility and without pride, but he felt that Taylor went too far in suggesting that each individual should think of himself or herself as the worst person in any company. He was also unhappy with Taylor's notion that we cannot know if we are forgiven by God. Wesley's argument was that grace comes through Holy Communion, and that this grace cannot be of so little a force that it is impossible to tell if we have received it or not. In the second letter to his mother the following month (29 July), he was stimulated by Taylor to set forth his belief that faith has a rational ground, in that he did not think it was possible, without perjury, to swear he believed in anything unless he had a rational ground for that persuasion. In the same letter he set out his objection to predestination, a view that he retained for the rest of his life, seeing predestination as inconsistent with divine justice or mercy.

Three years later he was again reading Jeremy Taylor, and discussed Taylor's *Holy Living and Holy Dying* in another letter written to his mother on 28 February 1730. Here he agreed with Taylor's view concerning the pardon of sins, which centres on the belief that Christ came to take away our sins, and that forgiveness of sin is a state of change effected upon us. What greatly impressed Wesley in Jeremy Taylor's work was the part of *Holy Living and Holy Dying* that related to purity of intention. It caused Wesley to resolve to dedicate all of his life to God: his thoughts, words and actions.[14]

When reading Thomas à Kempis's *The Imitation of Christ*, Wesley was confronted with the very nature of inward religion. He came to the realization that giving all his life to God would be worthless unless he also gave his heart.[15] This conclusion was reinforced a few years later when he read William Law's *Christian Perfection* and *Serious Call*. These books brought him to an important conclusion: that it was impossible to be half a Christian. He consequently resolved again, through the grace of God, to give his whole self to God.[16] His reading had not only broadened his outlook and introduced him to new ideas, but had also caused him to make firm resolutions to which he remained faithful for the rest of his life. It had also brought him to a realization of the power of the printed word, not only of the Bible, but of supporting devotional literature. He thus spent much of his time in later life writing tracts, abbreviating the Christian classics, and publishing sermons, journals and hymns.

Wesley's re-evaluation of his Christian life

Wesley's appointment as a Fellow of Lincoln College gave an extra impetus to the process of re-evaluating his Christian life, which caused him not only to review his use of time, but also his use of money. He resolved to pay off his bills and to live no more on credit.[17] Three years later, in 1729, he took on a curacy in order to supplement his stipend and to help to pay for his horse. The horse no doubt was very convenient, but the financial argument he put forward that it would save money on renting a horse seems less than convincing.[18]

As a young Fellow, Wesley took his duties seriously. In his first year he was elected Lecturer in Logic and Greek, and added to these the responsibilities of Lecturer in Philosophy four years later. When referring to his duty of care towards his students he said, 'I should have thought myself little better than a highwayman if I had not lectured them every day of the year but Sundays.'[19] He also took his turn to conduct prayers in the College Chapel or to preach in the city churches. When the Rector, Dr Morley, suddenly died of a stroke in his Scotton parish, Wesley took a leading role in the election of his successor. Wesley favoured an internal candidate, Euseby Isham, and spent a considerable amount of time talking to other Fellows to elicit their support. Isham was duly elected Rector in July 1731. Wesley joined with four other Fellows in a cross-country journey to the Bishop of Lincoln's Palace at Buckland. The purpose of the visit was that the College statutes demanded that the Fellows must seek confirmation of the election of the Rector from the College Visitor, the Bishop of Lincoln. From Buckland, they went on to visit Cambridge.

Wesley soon became a valued person in the Lincoln College fellowship, and an indication of the esteem and affection the other Fellows felt for Wesley was his re-election while he was away in Georgia from 1735 to 1738. This was not a straightforward election. Wesley's own fellowship should have lapsed as he had not fulfilled the requirement demanded of all Fellows of Lincoln (with one exception): that within seven years of being elected they take the Bachelor of Divinity degree. In his absence, the Fellows of the College elected him to the only Lincoln fellowship that was free of this requirement and thereby enabled him to continue as a Fellow of the College.

Wesley's social life at Oxford

Lincoln also provided John with a considerable part of his social life. Most evenings after dinner he would join other Fellows for conversation in the Senior Common Room. His closest friend was Richard Hutchins: the two would often go for long walks together, and Hutchins would almost always be present in St Mary's University Church when Wesley was preaching. When Hutchins stood as a University Proctor, in charge of student discipline and examinations, Wesley turned out to vote for him.

Wesley's social life, however, was not confined to the College. He gathered many friends around him from the wider university, joining them for breakfast in Christ Church or Merton, meeting in the Oxford coffee houses or gathering together in his room.[20] He generally had breakfast with others, he dined with others, he rarely drank tea on his own, and he often worked alongside other people. He was an outgoing and friendly man who enjoyed company. One group of young women friends who played a key role in his emotional and religious development were the Kirkham sisters and their friends, the Granville sisters. The Reverend Lionel Kirkham was the Rector of Stanton, near Broadway, overlooking the Vale of Evesham. He and his wife had two sons: Robert, who entered Merton College, Oxford, in 1729, and Bernard, who came up to Corpus Christi College, Oxford, in 1735. They also had three daughters: Sarah (or Sally), who was four years older than Wesley, Elizabeth (or Betty), and Damaris.[21] It was probably Sally Kirkham who drew Wesley constantly back to the three-storey vicarage at Stanton, and was the 'Varanese' of Wesley's correspondence.[22] It seems quite likely that it was Sally who recommended that Wesley should read Thomas à Kempis and Jeremy Taylor, after his visit to Stanton on 28 May 1725.[23] There seems little doubt that Wesley had fallen in love with Sally Kirkham, and that this had stimulated his interest in books of which he was aware but had hitherto taken little serious notice. She became a kind of spiritual adviser, and to some extent he seems to have been hers.

Wesley must have entertained thoughts of marrying Sally, but at the time of their meeting he had no money and many debts; also, he was considerably younger than she was, and marriage would have quenched any hope he might have had at that time of becoming a Fellow of an Oxford College. John did not propose to her, and in the last days of 1725 Sally married a schoolteacher, the Reverend John Chapone, and as far as one can tell she had a happy marriage and a large family. John Wesley attended the wedding at Stanton, and generously wrote in his diary a comment wishing her happiness. He was still very fond of her, and probably deeply in love with her also. The two continued to meet and talk about religion and theology; they also wrote to each other, but the letters sadly no longer exist. After she had been married for nine months she told him that she was sure that her husband would never resent the freedom they enjoyed. 'Later that evening as he sat with Sally and her sister, he leaned on her breast and clasped both her hands in his, and while her sister looked on tenderly, she said many "obliging things".'[24] At the other extreme, during the Christmas vacation of 1726, their conversations included the Roman Catholic Church, Episcopal orders, election and the state of the Church in the West Indies.[25]

What should we make of this relationship? Members of Wesley's family, and especially his mother, were very worried about Wesley's friendship with Sally and her sisters; there was certainly a suspicion that this relationship consisted of more than a religious friendship that was helping him to develop his spiritual life.[26] Wesley himself probably thought, as Henry Rack suggests, that he was being led through human affection to heavenly love, whereas in reality the reverse was true: starting with heavenly love he was being led to human affection.[27] Wesley was drawn to Sally because he saw in her an idealized Christian person, a model of holiness and virtue, qualities that he felt were lacking in his own life. Belonging to a group was always important to Wesley, and to belong to this delightful circle of sisters must have been both exciting and stimulating.

It was through the Kirkham sisters that John Wesley in 1730 met Mary Pendarves, the former Miss Mary Granville. To some extent she took the place of Sally Kirkham in his affections, although the three of them remained friends for several years. In a letter written to Mary Pendarves on 'Innocents Day' 1730, Wesley maintained that there was a close resemblance between the emotions he felt for her to those that he had experienced when he first talked and corresponded with Sally Kirkham.

Mary Pendarves was born in 1700 and was three years older than Wesley. One of her great-grandfathers was Sir Basil Granville, who was killed in the English Civil War while fighting for the King at Lansdowne. Her great-uncle was the Earl of Bath. On his retirement in 1714, her father came to live at Buckland near Broadway, which was two miles from the rectory at Stanton. It was here that Mary Granville and her sister Anne came to know the Kirkham family. While staying with her uncle, Lord Lansdowne, she met her future husband; he was 60 and she was 17. The two married, but he died when she was 24, leaving her a 'very mediocre' fortune, but a sufficient income for her needs. By 1725 she had become a charming, beautiful and eligible widow with her own private means. Five years later, in June 1730, she heard John Wesley preach and asked him for a copy of his sermon. His diary shows that he was staying at Stanton in July 1730, when he met her; he further noted in August of the same year that he was transcribing a sermon for her.[28] In the few years that followed their first meeting, John Wesley and Mary Pendarves carried on a correspondence that gives some insights into both of them.

The first letter written by Wesley to Mary seems rather too grovelling and over-grateful.[29] However, as the correspondence proceeded, the tone of the Wesley letters became more confident; he moved away from concentrating on his own inadequacies towards more of a preaching style, and then in the direction of giving sound advice. Throughout the correspondence he regarded Mary as an innocent and good person, compared to himself, and wrote that he needed her help in order to attain holiness.[30] As time went by his letters became longer, and in general her letters got shorter. He often wrote back immediately, whereas she was inclined to allow considerable periods of time to elapse before replying. Sometimes he wrote two letters to her one. Most people reading the correspondence would begin to form the impression that he was far more keen on the friendship than she was. It is also interesting to note that on two occasions she asked him to burn her letters when he had read them.[31] It seems odd that, although he complied with this request, before doing so he made careful copies of all the letters. Was he in love with her, and wished to keep the correspondence as a constant reminder of her, or did he feel that the letters were of importance for his own spiritual development? Whatever the answer to this question, it was strange that he went out of his way to comply with the letter of her request, but not the spirit of it.

There was a long break in the correspondence while Mary Pendarves was in Ireland. Shortly after her return she tried to restore the relationship and wrote to John Wesley in July 1734. Wesley replied in a courteous but firm manner and brought the correspondence to a close. Why did he do this? By 1734 even he would have seen that there was no future in this relationship. He was probably hurt at her long silence, for he wrote in his final letter that her silence 'did, indeed, deprive me of much pleasure . . .'[32] The most important reason of all was that his interest had moved on: with the activities of the Holy Club and a continuing desire for a useful life, the centre of his interests was changing. In a little over a year he would be setting off for the New World. One cannot help wondering if the conclusion of this relationship was one of the factors that propelled him into more religious activity here in England and later in America.

Oxford and the Holy Club

John Wesley spent most of the period from the summer of 1727 to the autumn of 1729 at Epworth and Wroot, acting as curate to his father. He also helped his father with his work on the Book of Job. He continued to read widely, preach and get up early to spend time in private prayer. Most Sundays he preached at Wroot, but occasionally he crossed the Trent to preach in the small villages on the eastern bank of the river. The slow and gentle life of the country parson was suddenly interrupted on 21 October 1729 by a letter from the Rector of Lincoln College, requesting Wesley's immediate return to Oxford. All the Junior Fellows were being recalled to give supervision and instruction to undergraduates, in order to help improve the morals of students within the university.[33]

Towards the end of November, therefore, John Wesley returned to Oxford to take up his academic duties. During his absence he had kept in close touch with the College, so he had a good idea of what was happening in the College community. One change he found on his return to Oxford was that his brother Charles was regularly meeting on Sunday evenings with William Morgan and Robert Kirkham to talk about religious books. These meetings were the result of a change in attitude that had come over Charles, who was now working much harder than in his first year. He was also engaged in private prayer at regular intervals in the day and attending Holy Communion. On his return, John not only took on the unofficial post of Charles's tutor in Classics, but also the role of Charles's spiritual adviser. He soon became the natural leader of the band of four that came to be known as the 'Holy Club'. Under John's leadership, and with the example of William Morgan, the Holy Club soon extended its activities into the areas of pastoral care. It was not long before the tiny group of members were visiting the prisoners in Oxford Castle, those in the debtors' prison, and ministering to the sick. In December 1730 they provided a sermon and prayers on Sunday, a Christmas dinner the following week, and Holy Communion the one after.

Throughout 1731 the Holy Club made great progress, but it was not without opposition. In July of that year John wrote to Mary Pendarves, 'I have been charged with being too strict, with carrying things too far in religion.' Although John was well able to answer the criticism, it was nevertheless hurtful. Worse was to come; in writing to his mother two years later, in August 1733, he said 'ill men say all manner of evil of me, and good men believe them'. According to Wesley's account, it was not long before rumours were circulating that one of the canons of Christ Church, Dr Terry, together with the senior tutors, 'were going to blow up the Godly Club'[34] in an effort to stop the progress of the Methodist movement. The criticism had been given substance by the death of an undergraduate, William Morgan, on 26 August 1732.

Morgan was a young Irish student who had been one of the original members of the Holy Club and an undergraduate at Christ Church. He not only encouraged the other members of the Holy Club to visit the prisoners in Oxford Castle and to care for the sick, but also started a school for the children of prisoners. His father, Richard Morgan, disliked his son using his allowance for charitable purposes and vowed to provide him only with resources for his health and education. William became ill in 1731, and left Oxford for Dublin, where he died on 26 August 1732. Early in September Richard Morgan wrote a letter to Charles Wesley in which he gave an account of his son's death. Ten days later John Wesley heard the gossip in Oxford that he and his brother Charles had been responsible for William Morgan's death, through excessive fasting encouraged by them. It was believed that this rigorous fasting had over the years driven William Morgan mad.

John Wesley felt that on this occasion he could not let this charge go unanswered, so he wrote a long letter to Richard Morgan giving a detailed account of his actions and of the practices of the early Oxford Methodists. Wesley's long letter won over Richard Morgan, who subsequently entrusted a second son to Wesley's care. Wesley later published this letter as a preface to his Journal. The letter not only set the record straight as far as the Wesley brothers were concerned, but it also gives a detailed and useful account of the early days of the Holy Club. In particular, Wesley pointed out that William Morgan had abandoned fasting one and a half years previously, while Wesley had started fasting only six months before.[35]

Initially the four members of the Holy Club had agreed to spend three or four evenings each week together reading the Classics on weekdays and reading a work on divinity on Sundays. When William Morgan had suggested they visit prisoners and those who were ill, Wesley wrote to consult his father and also sought the permission of the Bishop of Oxford through the good offices of his chaplain. Both gave their blessing to these activities. With this support the members of the Holy Club continued to meet together; they took Holy Communion once a week and did all the good they could for their acquaintances, for prisoners, and for a few poor families in Oxford. Wesley then set out a series of questions about 'doing good' that he believed encapsulated the spirit of the Holy Club. These questions fell into four distinct areas: (1) Whether all people should imitate Christ, who went about doing good. (2) Whether we should do good to our acquaintances. (3) Whether we should do good to those in need. (4) Whether we should do good to those in prison.[36] Wesley said that he did not approve of any person who answered these questions negatively.

Membership of the Holy Club was enlarged by the addition of John Clayton of Brasenose, together with a few of his pupils, and also some pupils of John and Charles Wesley.[37] Another important addition to the Holy Club was John

Gambold, who joined the Wesleys in 1732. He had called on Charles Wesley two years previously, and later Charles had introduced him to John. It is of some significance that in 1734 Gambold presented Charles with a 1613 edition of *An Introduction to a Devout Life* by Francis Sales, Bishop of Geneva; the book is now to be found in Harris Manchester College Library. Gambold at a relatively young age became the incumbent of Stanton Harcourt and later became a Moravian bishop. Several years later he wrote an eye-witness account of the Holy Club and in it described John Wesley as 'always the chief manager'. Gambold credits Wesley as being not only better educated than the rest, but also earnest and constantly the same.[38] According to Wesley's account, a small group of Holy Club members met on two evenings a week to talk about Wesley's great plan and to read books and articles on practical divinity.

During this period John Wesley's interests were beginning to change, and the Holy Club began to move towards the centre of his life and thought. He also gave great consideration as to how it could work outside the university, and it was not long before he was meeting for prayer in the town as well as within the university. His own lifestyle began to change and he set down strict rules for himself. He made several resolutions including the following: he would only drink one glass of wine or ale in the College dining hall; on fast days he would only eat a small breakfast; at dinner he would never taste more than three dishes; he would never take more than one slice of pudding; in the common room he would always try to help himself last.[39] Members of the Holy Club lived on the same amount of money each year, and as their incomes rose they gave more away to charity.[40]

As the leader of the Holy Club, Wesley emphasized three aspects of Christian life: (1) the central place of Holy Communion and worship; (2) the responsibility of doing good to all; and (3) the importance of the written word for both developing and defending the faith. It is not surprising therefore that Wesley started publishing books so that his message could reach a wider audience. In 1733 he published *A Collection of Forms of Prayer for every day of the Week*, and a few months later published an abridged version of John Norris's *Christian Prudence*. In 1735 he reprinted his father's 'Letter of Advice to a Young Clergyman', published a sermon entitled 'The Troubled Rest of Good Men' and an edition of Thomas à Kempis's *The Imitation of Christ*.

Two other events of this time made an impact on Wesley. In July 1732 he visited William Law at Putney and, following a conversation between the two of them, Wesley started to read *Theologica Germanica* and other mystical works. Although influenced by mysticism, Wesley was never destined to become a fully committed mystic. He was far more interested in duty and good works as ways of expressing holiness. We cannot be sure when Wesley finally abandoned mysticism, but he had certainly given up this approach to religion within a short time of arriving in North America.

The following month Wesley was elected a member of the Society for

Promoting Christian Knowledge. He thus continued a family tradition, for his father had been one of the early members of the Society. However, it was under the aegis of the Society for the Propagation of the Gospel that John Wesley was to sail to America to begin a new phase of his life.

Chapter 5

Georgia

In mid-October 1734 John Wesley received news that his father was seriously ill. He set out immediately to visit him, and although on his arrival at Epworth he found that Samuel was better, John decided to stay on in Lincolnshire for several weeks to help with the duties of the parish. On 16 October Samuel proposed to John that he should take over the living at Epworth, which he would resign straight away in John's favour. John would be able to continue his father's work of 40 years and, Samuel argued, the poor people of the area had a love and respect for him and would like him to be their minister. John consulted an old family friend, the Reverend Joseph Hoole, the Vicar of Haxey, who warmly supported Samuel's idea, but John decided to put off the final decision until after he had returned to Oxford.

On 8 November, back in Oxford among his familiar surroundings, John wrote to his father to decline the offer. Samuel, though, was not a man to be easily put off once he had made up his mind, so he sent John a letter on 20 November urging him to reconsider; he also wrote to his eldest son, Samuel, asking him to put what pressure he could on John to get him to accept the appointment. There then followed a stream of correspondence as to whether John's ordination vows applied to a College, or university, or only to a Church, as the two Samuels seemed to believe.

As part of the exchange of views, John wrote a long letter to his father on 10 December 1734, setting out in some detail his reasons for wanting to remain in Oxford. He described how in College he had many friends of like mind; they had the same view of Christ and devoted themselves wholly to God. He also had the blessing of solitude and the luxury of being able to organize his own time, as no one would come to his room, except on very important business, unless invited. In Oxford he enjoyed the freedom from care, his wants and needs being catered for by the College. Oxford also gave him the opportunity of being able to attend public prayers twice a day and Holy Communion once a week. Although Epworth would give him a wide sphere of activity, his letter argued that he should remain in the place where he was the most holy, for there he could promote the

most holiness. Moreover, he considered that the students at Oxford were potentially a much bigger harvest than the parishioners at Epworth.

Whatever arguments John was willing to put forward to his father, the
real reason why he did not want to become the Rector of Epworth was
that he had no intention of restricting himself to an obscure parish in
rural Lincolnshire, nor did he want his own ministry to be a mirror image
of that of his father. In refusing to accede to Samuel's request he was (perhaps
unconsciously) rebelling against his father. John was determined to be his own
man.

In the spring of 1835 John walked home to Epworth for the last time to see
his father, who died peacefully shortly afterwards. In death, as in life, Samuel
firmly held to his Christian faith. He had completed his life's work on the Book
of Job, and although he had not been able to persuade any of his sons to follow
him in his work at Epworth, he had passed on to them something of his
Christian faith, and his love of learning, as well as his strong determination. Both
Tyerman and Green[1] produce evidence that suggests that, with his father's death,
John wavered in his decision concerning the living at Epworth. It was too late,
though; the family would soon be scattered and someone else would be
appointed to the post.

Two years prior to the family debate as to whether John should succeed his
father at Epworth, a little noticed Royal Charter was signed by the King which
was to have a profound effect on the lives of John and Charles Wesley. The
Charter of 1732 established a small colony in North America to be called
Georgia in honour of King George I and to be administered by trustees. The idea
was that of James Edward Oglethorpe, who had been a student at Corpus Christi
College, Oxford, and had subsequently combined a military career with that of
being a Member of Parliament. Oglethorpe was a kindly man, later described by
Benjamin Ingham 'as a pattern of fatherly care and tender compassion'.[2] One of
the many ideas behind his plan for the new colony was to provide a new home
and a fresh start for recently released inmates from the debtors' prisons of
Britain. The new colony was to allow liberty of religion to all except Roman
Catholics, who were still feared in England and also in Georgia, where large communities of French Catholics had settled to the west and Spanish Catholics to the
south.

Georgia: the background

If Epworth was remote, Georgia was on the edge of the world, colonized by
German, Moravian, Scottish and English settlers, with large groups of Native
Americans scattered throughout the colony. One of the newly appointed trustees
was Dr John Burton of Corpus Christi College, Oxford. He had a particular
anxiety about the poor quality of clergy who were being attracted to Georgia; he
realized that if the Church were to thrive and contribute to the development of

this new colony it would need people of the calibre and dedication of the Oxford Methodists. He therefore approached John Wesley, who was in London overseeing the publication of his father's work on Job, which was later presented to Queen Caroline. A meeting took place between Wesley and some of the Georgia trustees, including Burton and Oglethorpe, in the summer of 1735. John Wesley had visited Oglethorpe's house in 1732, shortly before he had been elected a member of the SPCK.

His father's experience of the debtors' prison and his own efforts in visiting the prisons in Oxford made Wesley very much in sympathy with Oglethorpe's scheme. He also expressed his hope 'to learn the true gospel of Christ by preaching it to the heathen'.[3] Initially Wesley hesitated before committing himself, but with Epworth now closed to him, he needed a new challenge. Never one to be hurried into a decision, he spent some time consulting his brother Samuel, and then William Law, whom he had met on several occasions. From London he went to Manchester to seek the opinion of John Clayton, one of the early members of the Holy Club, and finally from there to Lincolnshire to ask for his mother's advice. Surprisingly, perhaps, she was unequivocally and enthusiastically in favour: 'Had I twenty sons I should rejoice that they were all so employed, though I should never see them again.'[4]

With this blessing John decided to go as a missionary with the Society for the Propagation of the Gospel (SPG) on an annual stipend of £50. At first he was tempted not to draw the money and live totally on the income from his College fellowship, but his brother Samuel persuaded him to accept his wages on the grounds that not to do so would be unfair to his successors. Charles accompanied his brother in the capacity of secretary to General Oglethorpe, who had been appointed Governor of Georgia. Benjamin Ingham, another Oxford Methodist, and Charles Delamotte, the son of a London merchant, went with them. John recorded the purpose of the group in idealistic and utopian terms: 'Our end in leaving our native country was not to avoid want, nor to gain riches and honour; . . . but singly this – to save our souls; to live wholly to the glory of God.'[5]

On Tuesday 14 October 1735, off Gravesend, the little party of four boarded the ship, the *Simmonds*. On board were 119 colonists, 26 of whom were Moravians, and 19 crew members. Immediately the boat sailed down the Thames Estuary, the little group of Methodists filled every hour of the day from four in the morning until ten at night with prayer, study and good works; and, in addition, John learnt German. Progress was very slow (probably due to contrary winds): they did not leave Cowes, on the Isle of Wight, and sail past the Needles until 10 December.

The voyage was dangerous and uncomfortable. The first great storm was on Saturday 17 January 1736, when a large wave burst through the windows of the main cabin and soaked all those present, as well as their bedding and their possessions. Wesley pointed out that the storm had the great effect of silencing other grumbles on board the ship. A second storm on Friday 23 January swept Wesley off his feet while out on deck, but again he survived unhurt. On Sunday 25 January a third, and even more violent storm arose, tossing the ship to and fro so that it was impossible to stay upright; every so often a great wave would hit the stern or the side of the ship, sending huge vibrations through the boat. At seven o'clock in the morning Wesley went to see the Moravian Christians. He had been greatly impressed by their kindness, humility and meekness, and their willingness to perform some of the most menial tasks on board without receiving any pay.[6] Wesley was fascinated to see whether this group was prone to the same fear that had gripped the other passengers aboard the *Simmonds*. He was soon to receive an answer, for in the middle of singing their first psalm the sea broke over the ship with such force that the mainsail was split into pieces and the water poured through the decks as if the whole ship were being swallowed up by the sea. 'A terrible screaming began among the English. The Germans calmly sang on.'[7] On enquiring whether they were afraid, Wesley was told unequivocally that none of them were afraid to die. On the Thursday and Friday of that week there were two more storms, one of which split the foresail. The beds being soaked with sea water, Wesley slept soundly on the floor of the cabin. On 1 February 1736 they sighted land, and by 5 February they had arrived at the mouth of the Savannah River. The next morning Mr Oglethorpe took them ashore where they all knelt down and gave thanks to God.

The Moravians' influence on Wesley

This voyage to Georgia has become a central part of the Methodist story. There seems little doubt that Wesley learnt from the example of the Moravians: to the young Oxford don they were a shining example of Christian service and trust in God. He would also have seen something of the corporate bravery that could be engendered through the singing of deeply religious hymns when confronting danger. Isaac Watts captured this feeling in his paraphrase of Psalm 46, which Wesley would have known:

> Let mountains from their seats be hurled
> Down to the deep and buried there,
> Convulsions shake the solid world,
> Our faith shall never yield to fear.

But Wesley was not simply moved by the bravery of the Moravians at the height of the storm. If this had been an isolated event it might have passed unrecorded once the storm had abated. Their display of character throughout the voyage was a confirmation of Wesley's observation that they were a band of people whose way of life approximated to his ideal of the Primitive Christians, and that they had shown in their lives the faith and practice and discipline of the first Apostles. This terrible journey also influenced the imagery in John and Charles Wesley's hymns. In the same way that the artist Turner got the sailors to lash him to the mast at the height of a storm in order that he could return to his studio and paint what he had seen and experienced, so for the Wesleys, storms and mighty seas became a key part of their imagery:

> With faith I plunge me in this sea,
>   Here is my hope, my joy, my rest; . . .
>
> Though waves and storms go o'er my head,
>   Though strength, and health and friends be gone,

Wesley learnt that not everyone on board ship was in favour of his religious and devotional life. One passenger, the son of a former Governor of South Carolina, complained that public prayer was a great inconvenience to him because he did not want to be present in the same room as the worshippers, but he also disliked having to stay outside the room in the cold. Thus Wesley had to modify his practice and come to terms with the fact that outside Oxford and circles such as the Kirkham family, he would meet opposition and indifference.

From the outset of this mission Wesley had always planned that part of his ministry would be directed towards converting the Native Americans. His hopes in this regard were raised by an early meeting on Saturday 14 February with Tomo-Chachi, who was the chief of a small group of Creek Indians, settled four miles from Savannah. They were some 400 miles away from the main Creek tribes. Tomo-Chachi welcomed Wesley and told him that he hoped that Wesley would not try to instantly make them Christians as the Spanish Roman Catholics had attempted to do; they would like to be taught before being baptized. This meeting seemed to be a promising start for his work in Georgia, but it soon became evident that it would lead nowhere. He was forced by the withdrawal of another minister, a Mr Quincy, to take on the role of minister to the settlers rather than pursue the evangelical work he had originally envisaged among the Native Americans, because Oglethorpe was keen that the settlers should have the major call on his time. In addition, he found the Native Americans of Georgia to be generally undisciplined and unreliable; with the exception of the Choctaws, they were, he thought, gluttons, drunkards, thieves and liars.[8]

It would be all too easy to see Wesley's time in Georgia as a failure. But this would not be an entirely fair assessment of his ministry in America; there were successes in terms of his relations with the Moravians, his production of a new hymn book, his laying the foundation for his 'Christian Library', and his setting up of an American version of the Holy Club.

What impressed Wesley about the Moravians in Georgia was their behaviour and the organization of their communities, which in his view closely resembled that of the early Church. On his arrival in Savannah he lived with them for some time and was able to observe their way of life in some detail:

> They were always employed, always cheerful themselves, and in good humour with one another; they had put away all anger, and strife, and wrath and bitter-ness, and clamour, and evil-speaking; they walked worthy of the vocation wherewith they were called, and adorned the Gospel of our Lord in all things.[9]

He also had the opportunity to be present when the Moravians elected a new bishop. He noted that the process, which was preceded by several hours of con-sultation and prayer, 'almost made me forget the seventeen hundred years between, and imagine myself in one of those assemblies where . . . Paul the tent-maker or Peter the fisherman presided'.[10] Wesley was not only affected by them as an impressive Christian group, but he was also an admirer of individual Moravians such as August Spangenberg, who had helped him in his spiritual quest and whom he called 'that good soldier of Jesus Christ'.[11]

Wesley's hymn book and the expansion of his reading

Wesley's main debt to the Moravians was that they introduced him to German hymns, which he translated for use by English congregations. Initially he trans-lated some thirty of the German hymns, including some of the great seventeenth-century hymns of Paul Gerhardt and Johann Scheffler. These hymns laid great emphasis on personal piety and individual religious experience.[12] With charac-teristic energy, Wesley put his love of hymns and singing into practice by assem-bling a collection of hymns for worship, which was printed by Lewis Timothy of Charleston in the neighbouring state of South Carolina. *A Collection of Psalms and Hymns* (1737) was the first hymn book to be published in America, and the first hymn book to be compiled by an Anglican clergyman. It contained hymns from a wide variety of ecclesiastical backgrounds and was the forerunner of a long series of fine hymn books that have greatly enriched Christian worship. Among the 78 hymns contained in the book, hymns of Isaac Watts were well represented. Wesley also included five German hymns which he translated himself, as well as hymns by his father and by his brother Samuel. The book contained three of Joseph Addison's hymns and six written by George Herbert. Wesley included seven hymns by the Roman Catholic, John Austin, which were adopted from George Hickes's *Reformed Devotions,* the work of a non-juring Anglican.[13] The book was arranged in three parts: Psalms and Hymns for Sunday; Psalms and Hymns for Wednesday and Friday; and Psalms and Hymns for Saturday. It was designed for both public worship and private devotion. Wesley altered the texts of some hymns – particularly those of Austin and Herbert – generally for the worse; but the book as a whole is a most interesting document, both as an indication of Wesley's thinking at the time, and also as an early example of the use of hymns in worship.

Georgia also gave Wesley the opportunity to continue his reading. Among the books in the small library he took with him to Georgia were two books by August Francke, *Nicodemus* and *The Life of Gregory Lopez*. *Nicodemus* was written for ministers of religion and contains the idea of the Church as the Body of Christ, whose strength, life and spirit is poured into the most insignificant member.[14] The example of the poor, despised Jesus should be the model for his servants, but Francke could not find this in his fellow ministers, and concluded that it was their fear of their fellow men and women that prevented this from happening. It could be overcome by making the object of preaching and service the simple truth that was in Jesus Christ and the Holy Spirit. This work appealed to Wesley because its concept of the Church was in line with his own. It also perhaps helped to deliver him in later life from the fear of his fellow men and women.

The Life of Gregory Lopez was about a man who had devoted his life to God in a spectacular modern version of the *Vita Contemplativa*. This man spent a large part of his life in the sixteenth century as a hermit living in a cell in Mexico, with only a Bible, a globe and a compass for company. In order to bring his life into line with the will of God he constantly repeated the phrase of the Lord's prayer, 'Thy will be done'. These words, for him, expressed the whole of Christianity. Lopez's life confirmed Wesley's view that everything depended on the individual's will being surrendered to God and constantly being directed to God in love.

An important development during Wesley's time in Savannah was a small meeting that began in the spring of 1736. The Society met once or twice a week to help and instruct one another. From this group Wesley selected a little inner circle which met on Sunday afternoons, when he spoke to them in his home.[15] This may have seemed an insignificant development, but when Wesley came to give an account of the origins of Methodism he divided it up into three periods, the first being his return to Oxford in 1729, and the third being the group of some 50 people meeting in London in 1738 prior to his conversion. The second period he attributed to the time of this meeting in Savannah where he was able to build on his original ideas conceived at Oxford.

Wesley's difficulties in his ministry in Georgia

During his time in Georgia, Wesley achieved some successes, but he was also running into trouble. Within a few weeks of founding his American Holy Club, he was asked to baptize the child of Mr Parker, the second bailiff of Savannah. Mrs Parker told him that neither she nor her husband wanted the child to be 'dipped'. Wesley was inflexible, and informed the parents that he would only refrain from total immersion if they would testify that the baby was weak. This they refused to do. They then found another clergyman who was willing to baptize the baby by sprinkling the child with water.[16] Although he had upheld his High Church principles, in obeying the rubrics of the Prayer Book, Wesley had made enemies and his action would return to haunt him in accusations made before the Grand Jury in the following year.

This was not the only trouble that John and Charles were facing during the month of April 1736. While John had been in Savannah, Charles was ministering to the congregation in Frederica. Mrs Walsh and Mrs Hawkins, two married women, confessed to Charles that they had both had an affair with Oglethorpe, the Governor. They then told Oglethorpe that Charles was circulating malicious rumours throughout the settlement. Both Charles and Oglethorpe believed their stories, which created a rift between the Governor and his secretary. It was not until John arrived in Frederica that the matter was resolved and the good names of Wesley and Oglethorpe restored. Sometime later John Wesley was summoned to Mrs Hawkins's house, where he asked the maid to remain in the room. Mrs Hawkins first pointed a pistol at him and threatened to shoot him in the head. As he grabbed the hand holding the gun, she forced him back on to the bed and produced a pair of scissors in the other hand, shouting that she would cut out his heart. A crowd began to assemble in the room, including Mr Hawkins, but not one of them attempted to intervene. Being unable to free her hands, Mrs Hawkins used her teeth to tear both sleeves of Wesley's cassock and tried to bite his arm. Wesley shouted at Mr Hawkins to remove his wife. As an ever-larger crowd had now assembled, he dragged her off Wesley, who went immediately to the Governor's house to make a report to Oglethorpe. The Governor sent for Mr and Mrs Hawkins and, after a long hearing, they promised to behave better in the future.[17]

Wesley still continued to harbour the thought that he could convert Mr and Mrs Hawkins, and make them decent sober members of the Church. What he had failed to realize was that although it was always possible to convert a 'knave', the same approach would have no lasting effect on someone who was mentally ill. Mrs Hawkins's rapid change of character seems clearly to point to this possibility. At times she was quiet and devout, at other times angry and spreading malicious gossip. She was violent and then prayerful by turns. The young Oxford clergyman still had much to learn.

In the summer of 1736 Charles returned to England to report to the Trustees and raise further support for the work in Georgia. Whatever the official reasons given for his return home, there is a strong suspicion that he had had enough of the New World and was keen to return to Britain. In his absence the care of the congregation at Frederica fell alternately to John Wesley and Benjamin Ingham. It was on one of these occasions in June, while ministering to the congregation, that John noticed William Horton, a magistrate, seemed very cold towards him. Wesley asked him the reason for his hostility and was told, 'I like nothing you do. All your sermons are satires upon particular persons, therefore I will never hear you more; and all the people are of my mind, for we wont hear ourselves abused.'[18] This must have hurt Wesley greatly. His ability to get everyone in his congregation to think that he was speaking individually to them was a great gift, but in this situation it had caused much unhappiness. Wesley, who was always calm under fire, recorded in his Journal, 'He was too warm for hearing an answer. So I had nothing to do but to thank him for his openness, and walk away.'[19] There are several other mentions of William Horton in Wesley's Journal, all of them showing him as hostile, except for the last meeting recorded between the two men, when Wesley, to his surprise, found Horton civil.[20]

Sophia Hopkey

Wesley's relationship with an 18-year-old woman, Sophia Hopkey, brought his ministry in Georgia to an abrupt end. Sophia Hopkey, who was engaged to a Mr Mellichamp, was a member of Wesley's congregation and a friendship developed between the two when he started to read devotional books to her. It was not long before he was reading to her passages from his Journal, and some of the hymns he intended to include in his new hymn book. They obviously enjoyed one another's company and went for walks together in the evening. Sometimes they sang together.[21] John knew soon after his arrival in Georgia that he was quite likely to fall in love, for he wrote to his brother, in Greek so that it could not be read by others, 'I stand in jeopardy every hour. Two or three women here, young, pretty, God-fearing. Pray for me that I know none of them after the flesh.'[22]

Alongside these two young people who were happy together, experiencing a heady mixture of sexual attraction and religious instruction, there was also an outside factor. Oglethorpe and Causton, Sophia's uncle, wanted to retain the services of Wesley in Georgia, and thought that if they could obtain for him some high ecclesiastical office and a wife, he would remain in the colony. When Wesley had to make the journey from Frederica back to Savannah, Oglethorpe suggested that Sophia should go with him in his boat. Wesley recognized that a journey with Sophia, and having her with him in Savannah, might be too great a temptation for him. But he rationalized his situation by abdicating responsibility for the decision to take Sophia with him, and by reminding himself of his own decision to stay single. Wesley filled the days of their voyage by talking to Sophia about Christian holiness and reading to her from Fleury's *History of the Church*, as well as reciting to her several printed prayers. In the evening firelight with the sky above them, Wesley asked Sophia about her engagement. She replied to the effect that if she did not marry Mellichamp, she would marry no one. Wesley then made a comment that may have come from the heart, but that was also most unwise: 'Miss Sophy, I should think myself happy if I was to spend my life with you.' She asked him to speak no more about this matter. Yet by Sunday 27 February 1737 their relationship had progressed further. Wesley wrote:

> Finding her still the same, my resolution failed. At the end of a very serious conversation, I took her by the hand, and, perceiving she was not displeased, I was so utterly disarmed, that that hour I should have engaged myself for life, had it not been for the full persuasion I had of her entire sincerity, and in consequence of which I doubted not but she was resolved (as she had said) 'never to marry while she lived'.

Immediately afterwards he regretted his actions and, although he saw her every day, he did not touch her again. Wesley consulted his Moravian friends; he even 'cast lots' in an attempt to come to a decision. Sophia, who had now rejected Mellichamp, gave the undecided Wesley time to propose formally, but when he did not, she announced her engagement to a William Williamson. But even then she gave Wesley one last chance, for when she and Williamson came to see Wesley she said, 'Sir I have given Mr Williamson my consent – unless you have anything to object.'[23] Sophia and Wesley were then left alone. Wesley almost brought himself to the point of saying 'Miss Sophy, will you marry me?', but instead he asked whether Williamson was a religious man. She repeated that she had given her consent unless he, Wesley, objected. Little more was said between them, although both shed tears.[24] When Williamson returned, John asked them both to assist each other in serving God, then he kissed them both and turned away.

On Friday 11 March 1737, exactly one year after Wesley had first spoken to Sophia Hopkey, she and Williamson set out for Purrysburg, where they were married the following day. When Wesley heard of their departure, he felt physically ill. He tried to begin his day as usual with prayer and singing, but then recorded in his Diary 'pain'. By mid-morning he was experiencing 'much more pain'. That evening he went to the Moravians to find comfort, but could talk only about Sophia.

The following day, when Sophia Hopkey and Williamson were married, was a wretched one for Wesley; he felt that he might die, and indeed later that day he even wrote his will. Wesley's pain and unhappiness at Sophia's marriage led him to focus on two issues that later caused him much trouble. The first was that the minister at Purrysburg who had married the couple had failed to publish the banns before the wedding. Wesley resolved to protest at this illegality to the Bishop of London's representative in Charleston. He also harboured the thought that, because of this carelessness, the marriage was not legal.[25]

Wesley seems to have felt that he had been misled by the fact that Sophia had told him that if she did not marry Mellichamp she would not marry anyone. He was incapable of making an allowance for a sudden change of mind. In Wesley's defence it should however be noted that Williamson seems to have appeared so quickly on the scene that it was difficult not to draw the conclusion that he had been in the background all the time. Moreover, there is more than a little suspicion that Sophia was using Williamson in order to bounce Wesley into marriage. The situation between the Williamsons and Wesley deteriorated over the following weeks, and on 5 July 1737 Wesley wrote a letter to Sophia setting out his case:

1) You told me over and over you had entirely conquered your inclination for Mr Mellichamp. Yet at the very time you had not conquered it. 2) You told me frequently, you had no design to marry Mr Williamson. Yet at the very time you spoke you had the design. 3) In order to conceal both these things from me, you went through a course of deliberate dissimulation. Oh how fallen! How changed! Surely there was a time when in Miss Sophy's life there was no guile. Own these facts, and own your fault, and you will be in my thoughts as if they had never been . . .[26]

Shortly afterwards Wesley excluded Sophia from Holy Communion on the grounds that she was guilty of wrongdoing and had not openly declared herself to have truly repented.[27] Sophia did not take her exclusion lightly. Her husband supported her and two days later instigated a lawsuit against Wesley for defamation of character, claiming damages of £1,000. A Grand Jury of 44 people was assembled by Mr Causton, the chief magistrate, who was also Sophia's uncle. Wesley was unhappy at its composition and pointed out that among its members was a Frenchman who spoke no English, several people who had quarrelled with him and vowed to get even with him, and many others who would not be sympathetic to his situation, including a Roman Catholic, an atheist, several Baptists, and other Dissenters. Not surprisingly, the Grand Jury resolved that there was a case to be answered. There were ten charges. These charges included speaking and writing to Mrs Williamson against her husband's wishes, and expelling her from Holy Communion. Among the other charges were refusing to baptize the child of Mr Parker and not declaring his adherence to the Church of England. On at least six occasions Wesley reported to the Magistrates' Court to defend himself, but on each occasion the trial did not take place. Twelve members of the Grand Jury issued a minority report which refuted the charges against Wesley. In the meantime fresh allegations were made against him.

On Friday 2 December Wesley finally decided that it was time to leave Georgia and return home to England. He informed the magistrates of his intention and placed a notice in the Great Square of Savannah, openly declaring that he would be leaving that province. Later that day the magistrates informed him that he must not leave as he had not answered the charges against him, and that afternoon they published an order which required all officers to prevent him from leaving. When evening prayers finished at 8.15 p.m., Wesley took a boat down the river and early next morning arrived at Purrysburg. The journey from then onwards was much more difficult; walking through dense forest and swamp, and on several occasions getting lost, it took Wesley's small party three days to reach Port Royal Island. From there he took a boat to Charleston, where he boarded the *Samuel*, which sailed for England three days before Christmas.

The voyage back was almost as difficult as the journey out to America, with giant seas and hurricane-force winds. But it was much quicker, and Wesley stepped on to English soil at Deal on 1 February 1738 a much wiser and much sadder man. His relationship with Sophia Hopkey had been very different from that which he had enjoyed with Sally Kirkham and Mary Pendarves. In his association with these two friends he had been the one on the receiving end of suggested reading, and the person to be included in the circles of stimulating conversation. He had idealized them both, and saw them as pinnacles of goodness and holiness to which he had not attained. Both of them were also out of his grasp as far as marriage was concerned. He viewed Sophia Hopkey differently. He saw himself in this relationship as the minister of religion and as the spiritual leader who might be able to bring Sophia to salvation. He was also deeply attracted to her and enjoyed her company, her conversation, and her willingness to learn of the religious life. His relationship with her was that of a master with a pupil, a situation that has always had its temptation to slide from instruction into love – as the story of Abelard and Héloïse memorably showed.

Wesley's relationship with Sophia was dominated by the fact that she was both available and unavailable. Sophia would probably have been delighted to have married Wesley, but there was a sense in which she was unavailable to him. It seems clear that she had given her word first to marry Mr Mellichamp, and then to marry Mr Williamson 'if Wesley did not object'. Whatever Wesley's faults, he was a man of honour, and if he genuinely felt that she had committed herself to another, he was unlikely to undermine that commitment. But in this relationship he had been indecisive and she felt slighted and rejected. It was a classic case of two individuals totally misunderstanding each other and both feeling hurt and aggrieved and blaming the other. Nearly half a century later, when he looked back at the break-up of his relationship with Sophia, he wrote of his feelings at the time: 'I was pierced through as with a sword and could not utter a word more.' The intervening years had enabled him to add: 'But our comfort is that He that made the heart can heal the heart.'[28]

An assessment of Wesley's time in Georgia

Although Wesley was undoubtedly guilty of acting most unwisely during his acquaintance with Sophia, and especially after her marriage, it would be unfair to accuse him of anything else. This certainly was the verdict of two close witnesses. The first was Alexander Gordon, the Bishop of London's commissary in Carolina. He wrote to the Bishop concerning Wesley, 'he might not be acquitted of some imprudence and unguarded conversation', but added that he believed

Wesley to be innocent of anything criminal in fact or intention.[29] The second witness was Lord Egmont, the Chairman of the Georgia Trustees. He came to the conclusion that, although Wesley may have been indiscreet, he had not committed any crime.[30] These assessments were accurate, although not very complimentary. At the other extreme, Wesley's friend George Whitefield was possibly far too generous in his appraisal of Wesley's contribution during his time in America: 'The good Mr Wesley has done in America is inexpressible. His name is very precious among the people, and he has laid a foundation that I hope neither men nor devils will ever be able to shake.'[31]

Wesley's ministry in Georgia, although not matching Whitefield's eulogy, did achieve a measure of success. The congregation in Savannah had grown. He had started a similar group to that of the Oxford Holy Club, which he had found was an effective way of developing people's spiritual lives. Indeed, it was strongly argued by Curnock, when editing Wesley's Journal, that the whole Methodist system was conceived and developed in Georgia: the circuit, the class meeting, the love feast, and extemporary preaching and prayer.[32] In addition, Wesley's study of the New Testament that he had undertaken in Georgia increased his attachment to the Primitive Church. In his later theology and preaching, the Early Church was a constant reference point. Georgia had also given him an opportunity to develop his interest in hymns, which were to become such an important part of his evangelical mission. He had met the Moravians, and especially August Gottlieb Spangenberg, who had played a key role in his own understanding of the Christian life. In the rough and tumble of the life there he had abandoned his leanings towards mystic writers, which he believed had nearly made a shipwreck of his own faith.[33]

Wesley made several assessments of what he had learned from his time in Georgia. These were first set down on board ship as he headed back to England and later after having arrived in London. His initial comments were of a disheartened and depressed man: 'I went to America to convert the Indians; but oh! Who shall convert me? . . . I have a fair summer religion. I can talk well . . . but let death look me in the face, and my spirit is troubled. Alienated as I am from the life of God, I am a child of wrath, an heir of hell.'[34] However, years later he modified this early assessment by adding a note: 'I am not sure of this.' He also amended his statement about being a child of wrath with the words, 'I believe not . . . I had even then the faith of a servant, though not that of a son.'[35]

On Friday 3 February 1738 February Wesley again set down in his Journal what he thought he had achieved. He had not only learned to be more cautious in his dealings with others, but he had overcome his fear of the sea and given many people an opportunity to hear the gospel. But the overriding sentiment of this entry is that of the providence of God overseeing his life, 'In all our ways we acknowledge God . . .', who will 'direct our path'.

Wesley's time in Georgia has often been seen as a preparation for his conversion. But the experiences he passed through while there – preaching, hostility, Sophia

Hopkey, the Grand Jury, and the Moravians – were not simply a prelude to his conversion, but all combined into an experience that, although also leaving him depressed, caused him to feel that God had 'humbled me and proved me, and shown what was in my heart'.[36]

Chapter 6

Failure and Conversion

Within three months of arriving back in England in 1738, John Wesley was to undergo a dramatic experience. The account of his conversion set a pattern for later generations of Methodists; the anniversary of his conversion was to become a special occasion in the church year when Methodists would remember the life and work of their founder. There were many factors in the background of John Wesley's conversion, but four in particular are worth noting: his sense of failure on his return home, his reading of the life of Gaston Jean-Baptiste de Renty, the still-powerful influence of his parents, and his meetings with Peter Böhler.

Wesley's sense of failure on returning to England

On his return to England, Wesley's life was overshadowed by the sense that everything he had tried to do since leaving Oxford had resulted in failure. He had set out for America with high hopes of doing something worthwhile for God and of making a major contribution to the spiritual lives of native Americans and settlers. Those high hopes had evaporated and his missionary enterprise had ended in humiliation. His standing as a clergyman had been reduced. His image as a man of action and integrity had been severely dented by the court case and the many slanders against him that had circulated throughout the colony.

In addition to these problems, he had had the emotional disturbance of the attachment to Sophia Hopkey. This sense of his life being in ruins was compounded by the attitude of the Georgia Trustees. On 8 February 1738 he gave a short account of the colony to the Trustees. Although he spoke highly of the Salzburgers, he was critical of the one hundred idle people who had left the colony after only one month. There was also an implied criticism in his observation that the colony had only enough grain to meet half the needs of the people. The Trustees were on the defensive, for Georgia was in difficulties. There were disputes with neighbouring territories, and a fear that Oglethorpe might drag England into a war with Spain. When on 22 February Wesley handed over to the Trustees papers in defence of his own conduct, scepticism was beginning to creep in, with Lord Egmont, the Chairman, recording in his diary that Wesley appeared to be guilty of indiscretions. It is not surprising that a month later, when Wesley returned to them his licence to preach in Georgia, they accepted it 'with great pleasure'. They were beginning to see him not only as an enthusiast, but also – somewhat unfairly – as a hypocrite who was disliked by the majority of residents to whom he had been ministering.[1] His unhappy feelings about the sad state of his life must have loomed large in the period leading up to his conversion.

A second important factor was his reading of the life of the French Count Gaston Jean-Baptiste de Renty, who was born in 1611 and died at the age of 38. He had first read of de Renty's life in May 1736, and this book was one that he often referred to and that he was still recommending to others at the end of his life.[2] De Renty was a Roman Catholic whose greatness lay in his devotion to the Church, his concern for his family, and his care for those in need, especially the sick and the old. Wesley was greatly impressed by his humility and his deep respect for Primitive Christianity. It was as if de Renty provided a model of the ideal Christian life that Wesley desired for himself. De Renty not only gave Wesley an ideal to strive for, but may also have contributed to Wesley's dissatisfaction with his own life.

A third factor lurking in the background of Wesley's conversion was that of the influence of his parents and his home at Epworth.[3] Having stood out against his father's wishes that he should take the living at Epworth, it is possible that he had set out for America in order to make amends. We know that his mother approved of this decision. Consciously or unconsciously, he could have also been fulfilling his father's ambitions: Samuel had often entertained the idea of being a missionary to the New World. Even though he had risked his life and endured great hardships, the fact that he had achieved so little would have added to his sense of failure and unhappiness.

The influence of Peter Böhler on John Wesley

A fourth factor in the background of Wesley's conversion was the influence of Peter Böhler, who was a special commissioner for the Moravian Church in England and America. He was nine years younger than Wesley: he was born in Frankfurt in 1712. His father wanted him to be a medical doctor, but Peter had been greatly moved by seeing the faith of a woman who had been condemned to death. He subsequently chose to study theology at Jena, where he met Count Nicholas von Zinzendorf, the German nobleman and befriender of the Moravians, who played an important part in his conversion. In 1735 Böhler visited Herrnhut, the Moravian settlement, for the first time, and soon after was appointed tutor to Zinzendorf's son, Christian. For a short time he was an assistant pastor before taking up his post as Zinzendorf's representative. Böhler was staying in London for several weeks before journeying on to America when he met Wesley. In later life he became a Moravian bishop and spent his last years at the settlement at Fulneck in Yorkshire, where he died on 27 April 1775, and where a simple square stone still marks his grave. Peter Böhler was a deeply religious man who had undergone a religious conversion, and he wished to encourage others to find the faith that he himself had discovered. Böhler was keen to mould Wesley into his own pattern of belief; and Wesley, who had all the hurt and humiliation of America behind him, and an increasing number of churches closing their doors in front of him, was in a state to be unusually receptive to Böhler's ideas. Böhler was also enthusiastic to extend the Moravian influence, and Wesley provided gateways for him into the Church of England and into Oxford, where so many students would become Anglican priests. Oxford had always held a fascination for the Moravians: it was one of the places they wrote to when they had originally experienced the Holy Spirit at their settlement at Herrnhut. The events leading up to Wesley's conversion are silhouetted against this background.

It was the influence of Peter Böhler that shaped the course of Wesley's life and preaching over the course of the few months leading up to his conversion. He first met Böhler on 6 February 1738 at the house of a Dutch merchant, Mr Weinantz. Böhler and a friend had just arrived in London from Germany and, as they did not know London, Wesley kindly helped them to find lodgings. After that they met frequently until Böhler departed for America on 8 May. In one of his early conversations with Wesley, Böhler convinced Wesley of his own unbelief and his need of faith. Böhler instructed Wesley in the words, 'preach faith til you have it'.[4] Böhler's advice must be interpreted as an exhortation to preach the little faith you have, and you will find that it grows into something more. Some three weeks later Böhler gave Wesley an account of his own life, and told Wesley that the characteristics of a Christian life were holiness and happiness.[5] Here again Böhler spoke to Wesley's condition, for throughout this period the one thing that Wesley had not enjoyed was 'happiness'. On 22 April Böhler told Wesley what he felt was at the heart of the Christian religion: 'a sure trust and confidence which a man hath in God, that through the merits of Christ his sins are forgiven and he reconciled to the favour of God.'[6]

Wesley was prepared to accept Böhler's view, but could not believe that this faith was given in an instant. He was willing to put this belief to the two tests of Scripture and experience. When studying the Acts of the Apostles he was surprised to find that nearly all conversions were instantaneous. However, he found it difficult to believe that such things happened in his own day. On the following day, Sunday 23 April, Böhler introduced Wesley to several people who testified in front of Wesley to their own instant experience of faith. At that point Wesley accepted Böhler's view, but asked him if he, Wesley, should stop teaching. Böhler responded by reminding Wesley that he must not hide in the earth the talent that God had given him.

During the four months between Wesley's landing at Deal and his conversion in London, his mind oscillated between faith and doubt, between a sense of

God's presence and a feeling of being totally deserted by God. In these difficult months he wrestled with theological doubt and failure as well as with a fear of death, which on and off had dogged his life up to this point. However, his strong sense of duty prevailed, so that even through this period of critical self-appraisal he continued to preach and exercise pastoral care over those in need.

Because of the growing interest in Georgia, Wesley received many invitations to preach, but he had only been in England a few days when churches started to close against him. On 12 February he preached at St Andrew's, Holborn, on the text from 1 Corinthians 13: 'Though I give all my goods to feed the poor . . . and have not charity, it profiteth me nothing.' At the close of the service he was told that he was not to preach again in that church. This pattern was constantly repeated. The texts he preached on were often to do with sacrifice and self-denial, such as Luke 9.23. There is no doubt that Peter Böhler not only influenced his thinking, but also his preaching. It was not long before his sermons included themes such as new birth and justification, but it was his forceful attitude as much as his radical material that offended his hearers and closed successive churches to his preaching.

On 1 May, John Clayton, Wesley's old Oxford friend, wrote to him expressing concern, and gently pointing out that it was his extempore preaching that upset congregations as they saw it as self-sufficient and ostentatious.[7] Clayton's kindly letter had little effect as the following week Wesley was excluded from preaching at Great St Helen's. The record in his Journal for that day is of especial interest in that he declared, 'My heart was now so enlarged to declare the love of God to all . . .'[8] There is almost a suggestion here that he was preaching to meet his own needs rather than those of the congregation. Later in the month, on Whit Sunday, he was excluded from three churches in one day: St John's, Wapping, St Paul's, and St Benet's.

Wesley's conversion

From 10 to 13 May, Wesley fell back into a period of depression. He wrote, 'I was sorrowful and very heavy; being neither able to read, nor meditate, nor sing, nor pray, nor do anything.'[9] However, Böhler's letter of 8 May, written from Southampton as his ship was departing for America, greatly cheered Wesley. In the letter Böhler had exhorted Wesley to 'Beware of the sin of unbelief; and if you have not conquered it yet, see that you conquer it this very day.' It is interesting that Böhler saw unbelief as a sin and that Wesley accepted such an interpretation. Eleven years later when preaching his sermon on the 'Catholic Spirit' in Newcastle, Wesley told his hearers that one could not just conjure up belief; what we believe is outside our control.

John's brother Charles was the first to be converted. He experienced an evangelical conversion on Whit Sunday, 21 May. He was ill and in bed, but was quickly cured and immediately wrote the hymn 'Where shall my wond'ring soul begin?' John continued in a depressed state on the following Monday and Tuesday, but Wednesday 24 May 1738 was a day never to be forgotten. On that morning, just before going out, Wesley opened his New Testament at random and his eyes lighted upon the words 'Thou art not far from the kingdom of God'. In the afternoon he went to St Paul's Cathedral, where the choir sang the anthem based on one of Luther's favourite psalms, 'Out of the deep have I called unto thee, O Lord'. The combination of words and music made a great impression on Wesley. In the evening he went 'very unwillingly' to a Society meeting in Aldersgate Street where one of the members was reading Luther's 'Preface to the Epistle to the Romans'. Wesley recalled:

> About a quarter before nine, while he was describing the change which God works in the heart through faith in Christ, I felt my heart strangely warmed. I felt I did trust in Christ, Christ alone for salvation; and an assurance was given me that He had taken away my sins, even mine, and saved me from the law of sin and death.[10]

What are we to make of this conversion experience? In one sense, it was typical of the instant certainty that is found in Puritan spiritual autobiography. In another, it bore the marks of Wesley's individual conviction. Its consequences were also unexpected. It certainly did not end his need to wrestle with the Christian faith. Indeed, initially it did not bring the joy and happiness that Peter Böhler had told him were the great characteristics of the Christian life, alongside holiness. Later that year John wrote to his brother Samuel saying that he had still not received the witness of the Holy Spirit.[11] In the first week of the following year he made an ever stronger statement in his Journal:

> My friends affirm that I am mad because I said I was not a Christian a year ago. I affirm I am not a Christian now . . . For a Christian is one who has the fruits of the Spirit of Christ, which (to mention no more) are love, peace, joy. But these I have not. I have not any love of God.[12]

This was the last great outburst of doubt about his own spiritual state. In the coming years he was to face outward dangers, difficulties and confrontations. But from this moment on he was far less introspective, and (to use the metaphor from his own translation of a German hymn) the anchor that he had dropped on 24 May seems to have taken a firm hold.

It is natural that anyone who has undergone a religious experience will see it from different perspectives when looking back on it at various points in life. This was true of Wesley, and it is one of the reasons why it is so hard to make a firm assessment of the significance of his conversion. James Rigg, writing a century after Wesley's death, argued that Wesley's conversion marked his move from the High Church to the Evangelical Church, and that Wesley the ritualist was transformed into Wesley the preacher.[13] Rigg held that his progressive separation from the Church of England and his renunciation of church bigotry and exclusivity could be traced back to his conversion. However, Wesley retained many of his High Church views – such as a central place in his life for Holy Communion, and his preference for formal prayers over extempore prayer – which he defended in 1749.[14]

Wesley was eclectic by nature and tended to take the hymns, liturgy, worship and theology that best suited his purposes. Rather than abandoning all his High Church views at his conversion, it seems more probable that he was adding an evangelical string to his bow. What his conversion did at the time was to bestow upon him a great feeling that he had been forgiven. In addition to this, conversion for Wesley seems to have brought the Christian faith into clear focus. It may not have been the strong turning point in his life that some claim, but it was of vital importance to him, and to subsequent generations of Methodists. It was a key milestone in his journey, placed at a crossroads where a variety of thoughts and feelings came together and pointed him forward along the road he was to travel.

Chapter 7

Growth and Development

The date of 1 May 1738 was a significant one for John Wesley, for on that day the Fetter Lane Religious Society was founded in London. This Society first met at the home of a London bookseller, James Hutton. Associated with Wesley in this new venture was Peter Böhler, who had previously tried to form religious associations in England but had been unsuccessful. It was a Society within the Church of England. At the beginning it was neither Moravian nor Methodist, although Moravian and Methodist congregations grew out of it. In common with other religious societies, it had rules of behaviour, discipline and member-ship. The aim of the members of the Society was to meet together once a week to 'confess our faults to one another, and pray for one another, that we may be healed'.[1]

Ground rules of the Fetter Lane Religious Society

Everyone wishing to join would be asked why they sought membership, whether they would be completely open with the other members, and whether they had any objection to the rules of the Society. Under Wesley's presidency the Society comprised separate bands of five to ten members who met weekly. After meeting for two months the band members were permitted to attend the larger group, known as 'the Society'. This new Society quickly outgrew Hutton's home and moved into a redundant chapel in Fetter Lane. The Fetter Lane Religious Society did not simply reproduce the pattern of other existing groups, but was eclectic, in that it took ideas from the Anglicans and the Moravians as well as Wesley himself. Many of them were modelled on the Early Church.[2] There is little doubt that Peter Böhler also influenced the Society both in its general spirit and its organization.

Once the Society was under way John spent some time out of London visiting the Moravians in Germany and beginning his open-air preaching in Bristol. He soon became very active in the Bristol region as director of the religious societies there, and built a meeting-house called the 'New Room' in the Horse Fair as a centre for this work. By June 1739, though, the Fetter Lane Religious Society began to show tendencies towards separation from the Church of England. Charles Wesley, who was in charge of it in John's absence, had struggled to hold the members together. When John returned to London from Bristol towards the end of 1739 he found the Society in 'the utmost confusion'. He showed great self-control and courtesy in dealing with this. The debates that followed were eventually to lead to a separation from the Moravians. His decision was brought to a head because during his absence a prominent Moravian, Philip Henry Molther, had joined the Society in October 1739 and began to teach a form of religious quietism, called 'stillness' (this will be discussed more fully in Chapter 8).

The Foundry Society

Wesley formed a new Society whose headquarters were located at the Foundry. The Foundry was a dilapidated building in Windmill Street near Finsbury Square, which had previously been used as a factory for the casting of cannons. Wesley obtained a long lease on this building and erected on the site a preaching house with a classroom. The northern end of the building served as a schoolroom and was used later for the sale of Wesley's publications. The premises also contained living quarters that served as Wesley's home for several years and became the centre of his London work. He later described the formation of this Society. At the end of 1739 eight to ten people came to Wesley in London and requested him to spend some time with them in prayer and to try to help them to flee from the wrath to come. They also sought Wesley's conversation and advice.[3] Following this, they came together once a week under his direction on a Thursday evening, and later many more joined them. This was the beginning of the 'United Societies' in London. The aim of the first Society was to be:

> a company of men having the form and seeking the power of godliness, united in order to pray together, to receive the word of exhortation and to watch over one another in love, that they may help each other to work out their salvation.[4]

Preaching services were held regularly, but care was taken to ensure that these were not to replace regular church services or the participation in Holy Communion at the parish church. The Society had officers, called Stewards, whose job it was to support the minister. The Methodist term and function of 'Steward' originated from the Foundry Society, whereby two members offered to collect money for the building fund. Their duties included managing the temporal affairs of the Society: they received subscriptions, administered the funds, and distributed money to the poor. They were to be frugal and save anything that could honestly be saved. They were not to spend more than they received and were to pay every account within a week. They were not to expect thanks for all their work.[5] It was this kind of economy, whether applied to Societies or individuals, that enabled people and the Societies to become wealthier and flourish.

The development of Methodist Societies

An account of the development of these early Methodist Societies was given by Wesley in a letter of 1748 to Vincent Perronet in which he described the development of class meetings.[6] The idea arose when he was talking to members of the Society at Bristol about how they were to pay off their debt. A certain Captain Fry suggested that every member of the Society should give a penny per week until the debt was cleared. Another member of the Society pointed out that many members were too poor to be able to do this. Fry then suggested that 11 of the poorest people were to be put under his care and that he would call upon them weekly and collect whatever they could give. If they could give nothing or only very little, he would make up their contribution from his own resources. Moreover, he suggested that the better-off members of the Society should do the same: they should each have 11 members of the Society attached to them. In this way the richer members would make up the inability of the poor to pay. It should also be noted that members were already giving one penny a week towards the relief of the poor.

Wesley was quick to recognize the value of dividing the Society into these groups. He appointed class leaders, who were to exercise spiritual oversight to about 12 members. These weekly classes at first had a disciplinary and caring function, that of 'watching over' one another, but the members of the 'class' soon came to experience the value of Christian fellowship that developed in the meeting. Wesley carefully set out the duties of the class leader, which fell into two categories. The first involved visiting every member at least once a week to advise, comfort and reprove, as well as to enquire about their spiritual state. On these visits the class leader would receive whatever contributions the members were able to give towards the relief of the poor. The second part of the class leader's responsibility was to meet weekly with the minister and the stewards, and report on any member who was sick or in trouble, pay over the money collected, and show the accounts. Some of the members objected at first to the class system, but John Wesley showed that his scheme was flexible and could be adapted to suit different situations. He thought of it as a prudent system and admitted its human and pragmatic origin, even though he perceived his Societies as being very similar to those of Early Church groups.[7]

Wesley set up quarterly meetings so that he could talk to individual members of the Society. He gave out tickets with an individual's name written on them to those who he felt were seriously pursuing the Christian life. Disorderly members were not given a new ticket and were thereby deemed no longer to be members of the company. Some members of the Society wanted to develop their Christian life in a closer connection with others, and so Wesley responded by putting these people into small bands. The purpose of the band was to give an opportunity for the members to confess their faults and pray for one another in a more intimate group than a class. There were also Watchnight Services, Love Feasts, and meetings for backsliders, as well as gatherings for special groups seeking for 'Christian Perfection', as Wesley called it. These were known as 'select societies'.

The difficulties of providing adequate pastoral oversight caused Wesley to appoint Thomas Maxfield to take care of the London Society while he was away. He had instructed Maxfield to expound the Scriptures, but had forbidden him to preach as he was a layman. When he returned he discovered that Maxfield had crossed the boundary between expounding the Scriptures and preaching. However, Susanna Wesley persuaded John that Maxfield had a real call to preach, so Wesley accepted him and he was authorized to work wherever Wesley should direct him. Soon afterwards two others were received as regular lay preachers, and so began a long and noble tradition that still thrives today. Maxfield probably expounded the Scriptures to a general congregation as well as at the private meetings of the Society; anyone could attend the former, but the private Society meetings were open to members only.

Gradually the work began to spread northwards. Societies sprang up in the Midlands, Yorkshire and Newcastle. By 1742 John Wesley recognized the need to have a uniform procedure for all Societies, so he drew up rules for the United Societies that were published in February 1743 over the names of himself and his brother Charles. These rules, as well as laying down the way in which the Societies were to be conducted, also contained instructions concerning the behaviour of the members: they were to do no harm to others; and, among other things, to refrain from fighting, buying or selling spirits, and going to law against a brother. They were to do all the good they could to the whole community, and especially to the 'household of faith'. They were to help each other in business and employ one another as well as feed and clothe the poor. Lastly, they were to take their religious observance seriously; they were to attend services of public worship and Holy Communion as well as observing private and family prayers in the home.[8] These rules not only gave the Societies uniformity and a programme for action, but they also set in place a code of conduct that was in tune with the desire for self-improvement. Those who observed these rules were likely not only to develop their spiritual lives, but also to move from a working-class environment towards a middle-class culture of thrift, probity, respectability and prosperity.

Some lay preachers began to itinerate from 1740 onwards. Societies sprang up and they were placed in circuits or rounds. These were not named after the local towns, but after the chief lay preacher or founder. Gradually a full circuit system was developed with travelling preachers. The chief helpers were known as assistants, and later were called 'superintendents'. They were established in 1749 and came to be known as Wesley's local representatives.

Another important development was the first Methodist Conference in 1744. It met at the Foundry and was entertained by the Countess of Huntingdon at her London home. It was a small affair consisting of John and Charles Wesley, four other Anglican priests, and four lay preachers who were invited to attend. This meeting reviewed the work of the United Societies and stationed the preachers for the coming year. After 1744 it met annually and grew in numbers.

Other developments that helped the growth of Methodism were the publication of collections of hymns and sermons. The sermons were published not in order to promote or safeguard a doctrinal standard, but simply as a defence against detractors – to combat accusations made against Wesley and Methodism. Almost every year John and Charles produced a new hymn book: *A Collection of Psalms and Hymns* (1738); *Hymns and Sacred Poems* (1739); *Hymns and Sacred Poems* (1740); *Hymns and Sacred Poems* (1742).

By the end of the first half of the eighteenth century many of the procedures, and much of the terminology that was to characterize later generations of Methodism, were already in place. A structure was needed so that Wesley could keep a control over the Methodist movement and prevent it from becoming a victim to the enthusiasms and ideas of every individual member and preacher.

Chapter 8

The Moravians and Stillness

In the months that followed his conversion, John Wesley was greatly indebted to the Moravians. He had admired them since his first encounter with the Moravian brethren on his way to America, and he was curious to meet Count Nicholas von Zinzendorf, who had given sanctuary to the persecuted Moravians at his estate at Herrnhut in Saxony. Wesley was anxious to discover as much as he could about the Moravian movement, its piety, worship and organization. Thus he set out for the Continent on 14 June 1738, accompanied by four Englishmen and three Germans. This was to be the happiest summer he had experienced since the long, blissful days and warm evenings he had spent with his family in Lincolnshire shortly after his election to a College fellowship.

Wesley's travels on the Continent

Wesley was impressed by the paved roads of Holland and the cleanliness of the towns, but was frustrated by the reluctance of inn-keepers to take in foreigners; he even joked about it, remarking that eventually they found a landlord who did them a great favour by taking their money in return for food, drink and a bed.[1] The little party made its way across Holland by boat and on foot to Cologne, where they arrived on 27 June, and which Wesley referred to as 'the ugliest, dirtiest city I ever yet saw with my eyes'. One week later they arrived in Marienborn, about 25 miles from Frankfurt, where Zinzendorf lived with his family and a considerable number of guests. Wesley was greatly impressed by the way in which the Moravian Brethren were able to live in harmony. He was full of admiration for the frugality shown by the German nobility, who appeared to dress and live very simply. The Countess was dressed in linen and the Count in plain clothes. This way of life appealed to Wesley – so much so, in fact, that when he came later to write the rules for the leaders of his Societies, he insisted that they should display a similar lifestyle of simplicity and frugality.

On reaching the university town of Halle, Wesley was admitted to the Orphan House. It was a huge building forming three sides of a quadrangle, which housed some 650 orphans and taught a further 2,350 children. The building had dormitories, a dining room, a chapel and other apartments. Wesley also recorded that the orphanage had a large annual income for its support, generated by printing, the sale of books, and the provision of medicines. He was full of praise for the whole enterprise and recorded in his Journal for 24 July 1738, 'Surely such a thing neither we nor our fathers have known as this great thing which God has done here.' The orphanage at Halle sowed seeds in his mind that later came to fruition in three of his undertakings: the building of his orphanage in Newcastle, which became the northern centre for his work, the huge publishing endeavour that funded so much of his church activities, and the dispensary in London which enabled poor people to have access to medical advice and supplies.

On 1 August he arrived in Herrnhut, which is about 30 miles from Dresden. Wesley was keen to learn from the Moravian Brethren and they in turn were pleased to welcome him. They saw this young, educated Oxford Fellow as a way of increasing their influence in Britain and in the Church of England. Wesley described the settlement as having woods on two sides, and cornfields and gardens on the other sides. Most of the buildings were on the main street that ran from Zittau to Löbau. It had a shop, an orphan house for 600 or 700 people, and another row of houses which tended to divide the community into two squares. At the east end of the settlement was Count Zinzendorf's house, a small plain building with a large garden for the use of the community.

Before retiring to bed on his first day at Herrnhut, Wesley joined the community for their worship (in German, which Wesley understood). It took a simple form, constructed around three hymns. They began by singing a hymn that was accompanied by other instruments as well as the organ. This was followed by the expounding of the Scriptures and a second hymn. The service was concluded with prayers and a few verses of a third hymn.

Wesley was greatly moved by much of what he heard and saw during the 11 days he spent at Herrnhut. He joined in the Love Feast, attended the Bible classes, and worshipped in the services. He was deeply affected by the four sermons he heard preached by Christian David, under whose guidance the community had been first established. Wesley went to a great deal of trouble to record carefully the testimonies of several of the leading Moravians. His note records Christian David's own remarkable testimony and his outstanding courage. Wesley carefully recorded how the Brethren nearly embraced predestination, but finally – through the influence of Zinzendorf – came to the belief that, 'He (God) willeth all men to be saved and to come to the knowledge of the truth.'[2] Wesley attended the funeral of a small child at Herrnhut and wrote in his Journal not only of the beautiful, simple pageantry surrounding this rite of passage, but also of the deep faith of the boy's father. He noted in some detail the rigorous system of education used at the orphanage, where children were fully occupied with lessons and had no holidays. When Wesley founded Kingswood School 11 years later, he established a similar regime for his own pupils.

Wesley left Herrnhut on 11 August and set off back across Germany heading for England. There is no indication at this stage that he held anything but deep admiration and affection for the Moravian Brethren. Not even he could have guessed, as he retraced his steps through Halle and Frankfurt, that within a few months of his return he would be locked in theological and ecclesiastical combat with these high-minded and strong-hearted people.

On his return to England, Wesley put his energies into developing the Societies in Bristol and London. Behind the theological dispute that was shortly to erupt between Wesley and the Moravians, was the issue of who controlled the worshipping Society in Fetter Lane. The controversy might not have come to a head if Peter Böhler had remained in London a little longer, or even if John Wesley himself had devoted his energies to London, rather than spending so much time developing his work in Bristol. Zinzendorf saw the Fetter Lane Religious Society as part of his Moravian expansion. He wanted a foothold in England to add to his European and American settlements. Wesley, on the other hand, clearly saw the Fetter Lane Religious Society as part of his Methodist movement within the Church of England; he was in no mood to back down, nor was he the sort of person who found it easy to play a subordinate role to others.

Philip Henry Molther

The tension within the Fetter Lane Religious Society developed with the arrival of Philip Henry Molther in London on 18 October 1739. He came from the Alsace region of France and had studied theology at the University of Jena. Like Peter Böhler before him, he had acted as tutor to Count Zinzendorf's son, teaching him French and music. In 1739 Molther became an ordained Moravian minister, and in the following October was on his way to the Moravian settlement in Pennsylvania when he stopped in London. This temporary stop-over turned into almost a year's residence before he was summoned back to Germany.

The members of the Fetter Lane Religious Society were keen to hear him preach. At first he spoke to them in Latin and used the services of an interpreter. But as his English improved, so did the popularity of his sermons. It was not long before the congregation could not be contained within the meeting house, and flowed out into the adjoining courtyard. Molther was not only a good preacher but was also an enormously energetic man, who spent the daytime visiting members of the Society in their homes and talking to them about religion. In the mornings he would meet with the bands or preach to the whole Society. It was difficult for Wesley to counteract Molther's charismatic influence, especially as it was combined with such energy and devotion.

At his first meeting with the Society, Molther had been amazed and frightened by all the groaning and sighing and shouting that the members engaged in as a demonstration of the Spirit of Power. For his part, Wesley was also upset when he arrived back in London on 1 November 1739 and met with a woman who had previously been full of faith and good works. She now told Wesley that Molther had convinced her that she had never had any faith, and counselled her to refrain from doing any good works until she had received the gift of faith. However, despite growing suspicions, Wesley and Molther were still able to co-operate. Charles Wesley was appointed to the joint pastoral care of the Society along with Molther; and it was at Molther's request that John Wesley translated J. A. Rothe's great hymn,

> Now I have found the ground wherein,
> Sure my soul's anchor may remain . . .

In a letter of 25 January 1740 Molther thanked Wesley for the hymn and went on to say that he preferred it to any other hymn he had ever seen in English.[3] The letter went on to imply that Molther was superior to Wesley, in that Molther suggested that Wesley still needed to have opened to him the mysteries of the gospel, and that this would help his preaching. Such insight, Molther argued, had already empowered his own preaching. It must have been hard for Wesley to remain calm under this kind of patronizing message, especially as Molther had been ordained only a few months previously. Molther's approach, implying that Wesley was lacking something in his Christian life, was a classic manoeuvre to bring the other man under his authority. Earlier Böhler had used a similar approach effectively on Wesley, but by 1740 Wesley was more sure of himself. In this case he also felt that there was an important theological principle at stake, that of 'degrees of faith'. The fact that in the previous year Wesley had taken a lease on a former cannon foundry suggests that he had even then anticipated the break up of the Fetter Lane Religious Society and was already planning for the continuation of his London work in another place.

Theological divisions between the Methodists and the Moravians

Wesley had started to identify the theological issues at stake as early as 7 November 1739, following a long conversation with Spangenberg, with whom Wesley had been friendly at Savannah and who had arrived in London on his way to Germany. Wesley wrote in his Journal for that day, 'I could not agree either that none has any faith, so long as he is liable to any doubt or fear; or, that till we have it we ought to abstain from the Lord's Supper or any other ordinances of God.' By the end of December that year, after several discussions with Molther, Wesley had a clear picture of the issues that divided him from the Moravians.

Molther held that there were no degrees of faith less than full assurance, which left no room for doubt, and that the joy accompanying the gift of God was merely a matter of human emotional feeling. The way to faith, Molther taught, was simply to wait for Christ and be still, and not to use the means of grace such as worship, fasting, private prayer and Holy Communion, nor to engage in good works, because no fruits of the Spirit can be given to those who do not have it. Against this quietist teaching Wesley held that there were degrees of faith before full assurance of faith, and that the joy and love attending such faith was a joy in the Holy Spirit and the love of God in the heart.[4] Moreover, Wesley was delighted to have found a woman who had been converted through receiving Holy Communion, which enabled him to demonstrate that the means of grace could be a converting as well as a confirming ordinance.[5]

These theological arguments led to deep divisions within the Fetter Lane Religious Society. On 19 April 1740 Wesley received a letter from a Mr Simpson and a Mr Oxlee, begging him to return to London as soon as possible because Fetter Lane was in great confusion.[6] When he arrived in London he was informed by Simpson that the trouble had arisen because Charles Wesley had preached a sermon expounding the virtues of ordinances, whereas Simpson himself held that unbelievers should have nothing to do with ordinances, and simply be still, otherwise they would be unbelievers for the rest of their lives. By this time Charles, who had valiantly ministered to the Fetter Lane Religious Society, had reluctantly come to the conclusion that separation was inevitable and that there was no middle ground where the two sides could meet.[7]

When Wesley returned to London in June he found that members of the Society were refraining from doing good works in order to increase their faith.[8] He made several attempts to restate the Christian position represented by the Bible as he saw it. His efforts culminated in two sermons he preached before the Society on 26 and 27 June. The latter sermon was entitled, 'Do this in remembrance of me', and in it he set down for the last time before the Fetter Lane Religious Society the true and false positions as he saw them. In July one member of the Society asked if Mr Wesley would be allowed to preach to the Society again, and after a short debate the answer was received, 'No, this place is taken for the Germans.'[9] Four days later Wesley read out a short statement that concluded with the words: 'But as I find you more and more confirmed in the error of your ways, nothing now remains but that I should give you up to God. You that are of the same judgment follow me.' He then left the meeting and was followed by some 18 members of the Society. Almost the next entry in his Journal reads, 'Our little company met at the Foundery [sic] instead of Fetter Lane.'[10]

When Count Zinzendorf heard of the separation he sent Spangenberg, Wesley's old friend, to mediate between the two sides. Spangenberg reported back that much of the blame lay with the Moravians, and that Wesley had been hurt by them. The Count gave orders that the Moravians must ask for Wesley's forgiveness. When this failed, Zinzendorf himself came to England to meet Wesley. The encounter took place at Gray's Inn Walks, with a conversation in Latin. Zinzendorf was aggressive and dictatorial, although it is doubtful whether Wesley would have ever gone back to Fetter Lane, whatever approach had been adopted. Wesley was tired of wasting energy disputing with the Moravians; with the setting up of the Foundry he was preparing the ground for an independent and unfettered movement within the Church of England. James Hutton described the final events of Wesley's leaving from a Moravian perspective:

In June 1740, he formed his Foundery [sic] society, in opposition to the one which met at Fetter Lane, and which had become a Moravian society. Many of our usual hearers consequently left us, especially the females. We asked his forgiveness, if in anything we had aggrieved him, but he continued full of wrath, accusing the Brethren that they by dwelling exclusively on the doctrine of faith, neglected the law, and zeal for sanctification. In short, he became our declared opponent, and the two societies of the Brethren and Methodists thenceforward were separated, and became independent of each other.[11]

In his detailed account of this controversy, Southey believed that Wesley later unfairly criticized the Moravian Brethren, but he also made the point that there were some among the brethren whom Wesley regarded with great affection, such as Ingham and Gambold: 'They made Wesley perceive that all errors of opinion were not necessarily injurious to the individual by whom they were entertained; but that men who went by different ways might meet in heaven.'[12]

It was sad that two enterprises that set out with so much in common and such a great deal of goodwill should have ended in such hostility. Gordon Rupp has reminded us that the only humorous remark to come out of this unhappy separation was from Hutton, who was asked by Lord Shelbourne, 'What is your footing with the Methodists?' The reply was: 'They kick us whenever they can.'[13] However, as an old man Wesley renewed some of his Moravian friendships and was always pleased to see Hutton and Gambold.

Chapter 9

Wesley, Whitefield and Predestination

In the midst of his controversy with the Moravians, Wesley entered into a new conflict with George Whitefield and several of his followers over predestination. This was a much more painful conflict for him, owing to his friendship with Whitefield; and potentially it was a much more damaging one for the Methodist movement. In the end it led to the separation of Wesley and Whitefield, to the breakaway of the Countess of Huntingdon and her Connexion, as well as the formation of the Calvinistic Methodist Church of Wales. These events can all be traced back to the conflict of the early 1740s which effectively split the Methodist movement into two distinct camps: the major group led by John and Charles Wesley, which was Arminian, named after Arminius, who taught that all people may be saved by grace; and the other group, led by Whitefield, which was distinctly Calvinist.

George Whitefield

George Whitefield (born in 1714) was 11 years younger than John Wesley. An undergraduate at Pembroke College, Oxford, he first came into contact with the Wesley brothers when he witnessed them walking through a jeering crowd on the way to Holy Communion at the University Church. He greatly admired their piety and courage. Wishing to join them, he sought out Charles and soon became an important figure among Oxford Methodists. He decided to devote his whole life to preaching the gospel, and while the Wesleys were away in Georgia he was ordained by the Bishop of Gloucester.

John Wesley was greatly indebted to George Whitefield and throughout his life always regarded him as a friend. In the early days of their evangelistic work they were of one heart and mind. Whitefield first experimented with field preaching and then encouraged the reluctant Wesley to follow. Whitefield entrusted all his work in London to the Wesleys while he was in America, and on his return was pleased with the result. Indeed, Whitefield was as well known as John Wesley in the early years of the evangelical revival. The closeness of their relationship can be gauged from their early correspondence. Writing from Steeple Ashton in Wiltshire on 13 February 1739, George Whitefield addressed John Wesley in fulsome terms:

> Honoured sir, how shall I express my gratitude to you for past favours? I pray for you without ceasing. But that is not enough; I want to give you more substantial proofs. Believe me, I am ready to follow you to prison and to death. Today I was thinking, suppose my honoured friend was laid in a dungeon for preaching Christ. Oh how would I visit him! . . . I know you pray for, honoured sir, your affectionate son in the faith, George Whitefield.[1]

Before going to America, Whitefield knew little of the teachings of Calvin, but while in New England he fell under the influence of a number of Calvinistic ministers, who recommended that he read the works of the Puritan divines such as John Bunyan and Richard Baxter. As a consequence, he came to believe that salvation depended upon election. However, the differences between the two men did not surface until after John Wesley preached a sermon on Free Grace to a congregation of some 4,000 people on Sunday 29 April 1739, in Bristol. The text was from Romans 8.32, 'He that spared not His own Son but delivered him up for us all, how shall he not with him also freely give us all things'. The essence of the sermon is summed up in the second paragraph: 'The grace or love of God, whence cometh our salvation, IS FREE IN ALL, and FREE FOR ALL.'

The thrust of Wesley's preaching was that Christ died for all and that all *could* be saved, although not necessarily all *would* be saved. In this sermon on Free Grace, Wesley held that the doctrine of predestination did away with the need for preaching, that it destroyed all holiness; and that it removed the comfort of religion – and that in the end it turned Jesus into a hypocrite. Predestination, more than any other doctrine, struck at the very heart of Wesley's message. In fairness to Whitefield, it should be noted that Wesley was writing against a very extreme form of Calvinism. In later correspondence Whitefield pointed out that these assumptions are not necessarily true. The sermon itself did not cause a great controversy at the time, nor in the weeks that followed.

Whitefield and Wesley continued to correspond, and when Wesley visited London in the middle of June, Whitefield went out of his way to show Wesley the area where he had preached with great success in Blackheath. However, replying to a letter of Wesley's of 23 June, Whitefield took the opportunity of raising two key issues with him. The first was to bring Wesley to task for his apparent encouragement of great emotion among his hearers, which often led to convulsions in members of the congregation while he was preaching. Whitefield's argument was that such scenes would distract people's attention away from the word of God and encourage them to look for visions and convulsions instead.[2] Wesley, on the other hand, believed that while some of these emotional displays were false, many were the result of the Spirit of God working in people's lives, and bringing them to a deep self-recognition of their own sinful natures. Charles Wesley was much more sceptical than his brother concerning this, and he always kept a large bucket of water in plain view of the congregation, ready to dowse anyone who made such noises. Whitefield's second point arose from the fact that he had heard that Wesley was thinking of printing his sermon on 'Free Grace'. Whitefield requested Wesley not to embark upon this controversy, 'Silence', he said, 'on both sides will be best. It is noised abroad already that there is a division between you and me.'

Early disagreements

Early in July 1739 Whitefield again wrote to Wesley. The whole tone of his letter is that of a man who was increasingly worried and upset. Among many other issues he raised with Wesley, was whether Brother Stock was excluded from the Society because he believed in predestination. He then went on to request Wesley not to release his sermon on predestination for the sake of peace in the Church.[3] Whitefield lamented that Wesley had already 'cast a lot' on this issue; this was a procedure that Wesley had adopted from the Moravians when he believed that there was no biblical or moral injunction to act one way or another, and that reason was equally balanced on both sides. On 19 July Wesley wrote a firm letter to Whitefield reproving him for listening to unfounded hearsay, and a few days later Whitefield replied:

> I thank you for your kind reproof. Henceforward I will beg of God to keep the door of my lips, that I offend no more with my tongue. I would not willingly have one unprofitable word proceed out of my mouth . . . I love you more for reproving me.[4]

Not long afterwards Whitefield set out for America, and so removed himself from the English scene until March 1741.

While Whitefield was in America he wrote a series of letters to John Wesley in which he urged him to remain silent over predestination. His letter of 25 June 1740 expressed his general feeling: 'For Christ's sake, if possible, never speak against election in your sermons . . . For Christ's sake let us not be divided amongst ourselves. Nothing so much will prevent a division as your being silent on this hand.'[5] In addition to his plea for silence in public, Whitefield discussed two key theological issues in this transatlantic correspondence: Christian perfection and election.

Christian perfection was one of Wesley's favourite doctrines, and it was certainly the doctrine that caused him the most trouble in his attempts to defend it. In maintaining it, Wesley was caught in a pincer movement from both sides of the Church; the doctrine was criticized by supporters of old-fashioned orthodoxy, as well as by those engaged in the new evangelical movement. What Wesley meant by Christian perfection was not that a person would ever be free from ignorance or error, or even temptation. He believed that Christians were called to love God with all their heart and to serve God with all their strength; this he held was Christian perfection, and at its best would leave no room in the life of the individual for evil thoughts and sinful deeds. There were biblical texts that supported Wesley's view, such as 'Be ye perfect as your Father in heaven is perfect.'[6] Whitefield's argument was that while he was not aware that any particular sin had dominion over him, he still felt the struggling of indwelling sin every day of his life.[7] In the light of this experience he could not interpret Scripture in such a way as to bring him to believe in Wesley's doctrine of Christian perfection. He quoted the Bible as support for his view – 'There is no man liveth and sinneth not' and 'In many things we offend all'.[8] However, it was not the doctrine of Christian perfection, but that of predestination, that was eventually to separate the two men. Early on in the correspondence Whitefield wrote, 'The doctrine of election . . . of those that are truly in Christ, I am ten thousand times more convinced of, if possible, than when I saw you last.'[9]

Although Wesley was strongly opposed to predestination, he was not seeking a fight with Whitefield. On 9 August 1740 he penned a carefully thought-out and generous letter to Whitefield: 'There are bigots both for predestination and against it . . . Therefore for a time you are suffered to be of one opinion and I of another, but when his time is come, God will do what man cannot, namely, make us both of one mind.'[10]

While this correspondence was being carried both ways across the Atlantic, Wesley was running into difficulties at home with regard to predestination. On 17 June 1740 a Mr Acourt was prevented from entering one of the Societies on the orders of Charles Wesley. He wrote to John Wesley, demanding to know if he was excluded because of his views on election, which were, 'I hold a certain number is elected from eternity. And these must and shall be saved. And the rest of mankind must and shall be damned. And many of your society hold the same.'[11] John Wesley replied, 'I never asked whether they hold it or no. Only let them not trouble others by disputing about it.' However, Acourt told Wesley that he wished to dispute about it every time he came to the Society because he firmly believed 'You are all wrong and I am resolved to set you all right.'[12] Wesley kindly but firmly told Acourt that with such an attitude it would be better for him and the Society if he kept away. The following day Wesley told the Society about this incident and urged them not to enter into doubtful disputations, but instead encouraged them to follow after holiness and the things that made for peace.

During Whitefield's absence Wesley published his sermon on Free Grace. Charles Wesley complemented his brother's work by writing a series of hymns against predestination, affirming the most characteristic belief of the Wesleys: that the love of God was for *all*. They were published in *Hymns of God's Everlasting Love* (1741). These were some of Charles Wesley's finest hymns, and probably did more than anything else to anchor the Wesleyan Methodist movement in Arminianism:

> Father of mankind, whose love
> In Christ for *all* is free
> Thou hast sent Him from above
> To bring us *all* to Thee;
> Thou hast every heart inclined
> Christ the Saviour to embrace,
> All those heavenly drawings find,
> *All may* be saved by grace.

And

> Father whose everlasting love,
> Thy only Son for sinners gave,
> Whose grace to *all* did freely move
> And sent Him down a world to save.

Wesley was also getting into difficulty with some of his close followers over predestination. In December 1740 he went out to meet one of his local preachers, John Cennick, who was returning from Wiltshire. Much to Wesley's surprise Cennick treated him in a cold manner. When he enquired a few days later the reason for this treatment, Cennick told Wesley that he could not agree with him because he 'did not preach the truth, in particular with regard to Election'.[13] A month later, while Wesley was preaching at Kingswood, he was approached by Cennick with some fifteen to twenty other people who belonged to the Society there. Wesley immediately tackled them for speaking behind his back. They maintained that they had said no more behind his back than they would say to his face: that he preached man's faithfulness and not the faithfulness of God. Wesley was quick to point out that he believed that there was righteousness in man 'after the righteousness of Christ is invested in him through faith'. As the confrontation progressed, Wesley rebuked Cennick for making private accusations against him and separating friends from one another. When Cennick denied this, Wesley produced a letter that Cennick had written to Whitefield containing the following passage: 'With Universal Redemption brother Charles pleases the world; brother John follows him in everything. I believe no atheist can more preach against predestination than they.'[14]

While preaching at Bristol Wesley discovered that Cennick and other members of the Kingswood Society had formed themselves into a separate Society which held additional meetings 'to confirm one another in those truths' which they believed Wesley had spoken against.[15] On 6 March 1741 Wesley decided to bring the issue to a head. He laid before Cennick and his associates three charges: (1) despising the ministers of God; (2) not speaking or praying when first meeting together; and (3) dividing themselves from their brothers. He believed that the only way forward was for people to join one Society or another. When one of the group, Thomas Bissicks, stated that it was only because they held the doctrine of election that Wesley wished to separate from them, Wesley replied that this was not the case and that there were several predestinarians among the Societies in London and Bristol, 'nor did I yet put anyone out of either because he held that opinion'.[16] The breakaway party offered to dissolve their group if Wesley would re-employ Mr Cennick. But Wesley pointed out that Cennick had wronged him and failed to repent. After a brief period of prayer, Cennick left and about six people followed him.

Whitefield, although still not back from America, continued to be dragged into the predestination dispute. Early in January Cennick had written to him, begging him to return to England as soon as possible to redress the balance against Charles Wesley, who had become popular through his views on 'Universal Redemption'.[17] Moreover, a private letter from Whitefield to Wesley supporting the doctrine of election had been printed without either's knowledge or consent, and distributed to the members of the Foundry congregation on Sunday 1 February 1741. Wesley, believing that it was what Whitefield would have done, took his own copy of the letter and tore it up in front of the congregation, and all those present did the same.

In March 1741 Whitefield landed back in England, and Wesley resolved to see him. The meeting, which took place on 28 March 1741, was very short and direct. Whitefield refused to extend to Wesley the hand of fellowship and told Wesley bluntly that they preached two different gospels and that therefore he would not join with him.[18] This meeting effectively brought an end to their close co-operation. Clearly, Wesley and Whitefield were deeply divided on a matter of doctrine. Wesley commented on the split five years later, in his correspondence with John Smith. He protested against linking his and Whitefield's names together since they differed so widely. Obviously the name 'Methodist' was being used at the time to cover both indiscriminately.[19]

Wesley's attempts to be reconciled with Whitefield

Over the years that followed their separation, Wesley made several efforts to re-unite with Whitefield. In the summer of 1742 he made a list of items concerning election, over which they disagreed. He thought this exercise might be helpful in bringing them together. It can be seen from the list that he was willing to make surprising concessions to Whitefield:

That God, before the foundation of the world, did unconditionally elect certain persons to do certain works, as Paul to preach the gospel: That he has unconditionally elected some nations to receive peculiar privileges, the

Jewish nation in particular: That he has unconditionally elected some nations to hear the gospel, as England and Scotland now, and many others in past ages: That he has unconditionally elected some persons to many peculiar advantages, both with regard to temporal and spiritual things: And I do not deny (though I cannot prove it so) that He has unconditionally elected some persons [thence eminently styled 'The Elect'] to eternal glory. But I cannot believe, That all those who are not thus elected to glory must perish everlastingly; or That there is one soul on earth who has not, [nor] ever had a possibility of escaping eternal damnation.[20]

In the years that followed, Wesley kept in touch with Whitefield and from time to time made an effort to re-unite with him. On 1 September 1748 he wrote to Whitefield suggesting reunion.[21] In the following year he arranged a conference with his brother Charles, Whitefield and Howell Harris, but it came to nothing. In small ways the two did co-operate and occasionally preached for each other, such as on 19 January 1750 when Wesley and Whitefield together took the service at West Street Chapel. Another attempt to improve co-operation between Wesley and Whitefield resulted in a meeting during the summer of 1766 between Whitefield, the Countess of Huntingdon, and the Wesley brothers. The conference was an attempt to unite the various branches of Methodism, and the agreement they came to was that all the Countess's chapels were to be administered by the Wesleys, Whitefield and the Countess, and Whitefield was free to preach among all the Methodist Societies. For a time they were able to paper over the large cracks between the Arminian and Calvinistic Methodists, but with Whitefield's death in 1770 the chasm once more opened up.

It was a true mark of esteem that when Whitefield was once asked by a Calvinist friend whether they would see Wesley in heaven, he replied that he did not think so because Wesley would be so near the throne and they would be at the back of the crowd. It was also a great mark of affection that Whitefield had requested in his will that Wesley should preach his funeral sermon. In that sermon he spoke of Whitefield as a man of a catholic spirit, 'one who loves as friends, as brethren in the Lord . . . all, of whatever opinion, mode of worship, or congregation, who believe in the Lord Jesus; who love God and man'.[22] His generosity was typical, and it suggests that between the two men there were ties of love and affection that were deeper than their doctrinal differences.

Chapter 10

Preaching and the Preacher

There is a short note in John Wesley's Journal for Friday 24 August 1744: 'I preached, I suppose the last time, at St Mary's. Be it so.' He was referring to the University Church of St Mary the Virgin in Oxford, and the event was his farewell to his *alma mater*. After a brief comment he added, 'I left Oxford about noon and preached at Wycombe in the evening.' In his Journal, Charles Wesley gave an account of the event: 'At ten I walked with my brother and Mr Piers and Meriton to St Mary's where my brother bore his testimony before a crowded audience . . . Some of the Heads stood up the whole time and fixed their eyes on him.'[1]

This sermon brought to an end John Wesley's active relationship with the University of Oxford, although he did not resign his fellowship at Lincoln College until his marriage in 1751. Wesley's 1744 sermon, entitled 'Scriptural Christianity', had not been hurriedly written and speedily delivered, but was the result of careful and considered thought. He had proposed to deliver a sermon on a similar theme to the university as early as 1741. Among the papers discovered after his death was a manuscript sermon of 24 June 1741 on the text 'How is the faithful city become a harlot?' It appears that this sermon was written for the university, but never delivered owing to the intervention of the Countess of Huntingdon, who thought that it would be too controversial and create unnecessary hostility.[2]

Wesley's last university sermon

Three years later, the University Church contained a large and expectant congregation which included the vice-chancellor, the proctors, most of the Heads of Colleges and a great crowd of people from the city and the university. In his eyewitness account, Benjamin Kennicott, an undergraduate at the time, described Wesley as neither tall nor fat, and with black smooth hair parted exactly down the middle. Wesley's great composure, together with the fact that he spoke slowly, greatly impressed Kennicott.[3] In the sermon Wesley described a Scriptural

Christianity, in which righteousness, justice and mercy are to be found: 'Their love is without dissimulation: . . . that whosoever desires may look into their hearts, and see that only love and God are there.'[4]

Before asking awkward questions of his congregation, Wesley stated that it was necessary for someone to speak plainly to those present and then added, 'Let me ask you then in tender love and the spirit of meekness . . .'; he then went on to put rhetorical questions about pride and haughtiness, peevishness and sloth, gluttony, sensuality and uselessness; the consequences of these, he thought, might result in many of his hearers trifling with God and with one another.[5] He then tried to compare the description he had given with his view of Scriptural Christianity:

> Do ye, brethren, abound in the fruits of the Spirit, in lowliness of mind, in self-denial, and mortification, in seriousness and composure of spirit, in patience, meekness, sobriety, temperance, and in unwearied, restless endeavours to do good in every kind unto all men, to relieve their outward wants, and to bring their souls to the true knowledge and love of God? Is this the general character of Fellows of Colleges? I fear it is not.[6]

At the end of the service a little band of four Methodist clergymen, Meriton, Piers, John and Charles Wesley, walked out of the church in formation and none of the other members of the congregation dared to join them.[7]

Immediately following the service, the vice-chancellor sent for Wesley's sermon notes and Wesley handed them over. He commented with a little bravado in his Journal that the sermon would perhaps be read more than once by every great man in the university, whereas in different circumstances it would have gone without notice.[8] The vice-chancellor did not ban him from preaching before the university in the future. Wesley was simply not asked to preach again, and when it was his turn the university paid someone else to preach in his place.

Although Kennicott said that he had heard that the Heads of Houses intended to show their resentment, the Dean of Christ Church, Dr Conybeare, generously commented: 'John Wesley will always be thought of as a man of sound sense, though an enthusiast.'[9]

Why did Wesley preach this sermon, which he must have known would bring to an end his active participation in university life? In his Journal he maintained, 'I am now clear of the blood of these men. I have fully delivered my soul.'[10] It is true that there were many abuses taking place in the university at that time – overeating, excess drinking, rioting, struggles with authority and sexual licence. There were students who were not being properly taught and statutes that were not obeyed.[11] But this was not the whole story. Oxford produced many hard-working and able scholars in the eighteenth century – Joseph Addison, Edmund Gibbon, Samuel Johnson, Joseph Warton, Thomas Warton and Robert Lowth, to name but a few. There were also many conscientious tutors who did their best to teach and encourage students. In 1726 the Heads of Houses had put pressure on the vice-chancellor, Dr Butler, to send a letter to College tutors requesting them to remind all students of their Christian duty, and to recommend frequent and careful reading of the Scriptures.[12]

There was more to the preaching of this sermon on 'Scriptural Christianity' than Wesley simply acquitting himself of his duty to beseech members of the university to give up their idle ways. If his sole intention had been to change and reform the university, then a determined man like Wesley would have stuck at it for much longer. It appears more likely that there were other concerns coming into his life and that his interest had moved on. His primary attention was now on the world, which he famously saw as his parish. Only a few days previously he had held his first Conference of Preachers, which appears to have been a great success. He was also preaching to vast numbers outside the university, and he must have judged that the time had come to move away from the university, on to a more challenging and more dangerous enterprise.

Open-air preaching

Five years before his last sermon in St Mary's, Wesley had made the momentous decision to preach in the open air. This move came about through the influence of Howell Harris and George Whitefield. Harris was born in Trevecca, mid-Wales, in 1714. He came up to Oxford in 1735, but only survived one term before returning to Wales, where he began visiting people in their homes and talking to them about the religious life; when they gathered together he started preaching to them in the open air. Early in 1739, at Cardiff, he met Whitefield, who was greatly interested to hear of Harris's work and later reported that he found him to be 'a burning and shining light'.[13] When Whitefield arrived in the Bristol area in early February he discovered that nearly all the churches were closed to him, although the incumbents of St Werburgh's and St Mary Redcliffe were willing to allow him to preach in their churches. However, they were overruled by the chancellor of the Bristol diocese, who complained that Whitefield had no licence to preach and threatened that if he continued this illegal activity he would be suspended and expelled. Whitefield immediately decided to follow Harris's example, and on 17 February he preached at Kingswood to an open-air assembly of some 200 miners.

At a second service Whitefield estimated that there were 2,000 people present, and at a third service this number had doubled. On the fifth occasion that he preached in the open air he estimated that 10,000 people were in the congregation. Even allowing for the natural inclination of preachers to inflate congregational numbers, there is no doubt that Whitefield had discovered a real need among members of the community, as well as stimulating an interest. To see a clergyman preaching in the open air in full clerical dress, with gown and bands, was unusual in the eighteenth century, but to hear this young educated minister, with a real passion and fire about his message, must have been compelling.

In March 1739 Whitefield wrote to Wesley pleading with him to come to Bristol and continue the work of open-air preaching. In a postscript to the letter, dated 23 March, Whitefield added, 'I beseech you, come next week; it is advertised in this day's journal . . . The people expect you much . . .'[14] It does seem to have been premature to advertise Wesley's arrival in Bristol even before he had accepted the invitation. Indeed, he was not at all sure that he wanted to go to Bristol to preach in the open air anyway. Both his brothers, Charles and Samuel, were against the proposal, and there was deep division among the members of the Fetter Lane Religious Society over his leaving London. A further concern for Wesley seems to have been his state of health. The pressure under which he had been working led him to wonder if his strength would last much longer, and this concern had turned his thoughts towards death.

These worries caused him to hesitate until 28 March, when he finally won approval of the Fetter Lane Religious Society, but only by resorting to the New Testament practice of drawing lots. It seems strange that someone as rational as Wesley should have adopted this method of resolving a controversy. But an equally questionable practice (though quite common) was to follow, when members of the Fetter Lane Religious Society sought guidance for this venture by opening the Bible at random and seizing the first text that came to light. Wesley did, however, have the sensitivity simply to record the text in his Journal ('Now there was a long war between the house of Saul and the house of David: but David waxed stronger and stronger and the house of Saul waxed weaker and weaker', 2 Samuel 3.1) and not try to interpret it as a message for his new undertaking.

On Thursday 29 March 1739 Wesley left London for Bristol to enter into a new period of his work, which was to change both his life and the lives of those he encountered over the next half century. The journey was a slow one by Wesley's usual standards: it appears that he was in no hurry to get to Bristol. Before setting out he prayed, sang, met with people and conducted business, and on the way he meditated. He arrived at Egham by 1 p.m. for a meal, and at 8.30 p.m. had reached Basingstoke, where he joined others for conversation, tea, prayer, Bible study and singing before going to bed at 11 p.m. On the Friday he set off at 5.45 a.m., and that evening arrived in Marlborough. The following day he got to Bristol by 7 p.m. and noted in his diary that his horse was tired. It is impressive to see the number of people he met on the way – some were old friends on whom he called, and others were just casual acquaintances whom he engaged in conversation. In his Journal for that day he summed up his concerns about field preaching:

In the evening I reached Bristol, and met Mr Whitefield there. I could scarce reconcile myself at first to this strange way of preaching in the fields, of which he set me an example on Sunday: having been all my life (till very lately) so tenacious of every point relating to decency and order, that I should have thought the saving of souls almost a sin if it had not been done in a church.[15]

On the Saturday and Sunday Wesley went to hear Whitefield preach in the open air. Although there is some discrepancy between the Journal and the Diary, it appears that Whitefield set off for Gloucestershire in the early afternoon via Kingswood, while Wesley preached outside the city in a brickyard, to a teatime congregation estimated as three thousand. His Journal entry for that day reads: 'At four in the afternoon I submitted to be more vile, and proclaimed in the highways the glad tidings of salvation, speaking from a little eminence in a ground adjoining to the city to about three thousand people.'[16]

From this time onwards he was constantly preaching in the open air. On the Wednesday, at Baptist Mills, about one and a half miles from Bristol, he preached to 1,500 people. The following Sunday at 7 a.m. he preached to 1,000 people in Bristol and later to some 1,500 people at Kingswood. Although he lacked the fire of Whitefield, there is no doubt that Wesley was a very effective open-air preacher. John Hampson, who knew both Wesley and Whitefield, drew a vivid contrast of their preaching styles: Wesley exhibited 'the calm equal flow of a placid stream, gliding gently within its banks, without the least ruffle or agitation upon its surface, whereas Whitefield alternately thundered and lightened upon his audience'.[17]

Whatever his inner feelings, Wesley's cool, calm external appearance was of enormous help in his outdoor preaching; he exuded the confidence of a good ship's captain who authoritatively assures the passengers and crew that the ship will not sink. This outward appearance of being in charge brought with it the ability both to silence congregations and later to deal with the mobs. Twice on 18 October 1749 he quietened the mob – first, in Rochdale when he leaned out from a window to preach into the street, and second, in Bolton, where he remarked that 'the Lions of Rochdale are like lambs in comparison to those of Bolton'. Here, as the mob broke into the house, he called for a chair and stood on it to address the assembly: 'They were amazed, they were ashamed, they were melted down, they devoured every word.'[18] He not only had the ability to quieten the mob, but he was also exceptionally brave. He inherited from his father, Gordon Rupp suggested, the ability to look the mob in the eye.[19]

Wesley was also a good actor, and good actors can make good preachers. Horace Walpole was once among his hearers at the Countess of Huntingdon's Chapel in Bath, and he thought that Wesley was an actor like Garrick, although he seemed less impressed with Wesley's preaching style.[20] He had the actor's ability to set the scene, use his props, hold his audiences, and ad lib when necessary.

England in the eighteenth century, in spite of the misery and poverty, was a green and beautiful land and the backdrops for Wesley's sermons were some of the most lovely pastoral scenes in England: the wolds of Lincolnshire, the Pennine hills of the north, the rolling Cotswold countryside, the open skies of the eastern counties, and the valleys of Weardale and Teesdale. Sometimes he would stand under a great oak tree in Leicester, or preach in a ruined abbey near Blanchland in County Durham, or speak at the Gwennap pit in Cornwall with his back to the setting sun on a lovely summer evening: 'I stood on the wall in the calm of the evening with the setting sun behind me.' Wesley used his props carefully in order to see his congregation, and be seen and heard by them. He would climb on tables and chairs, walls and steps of buildings, village crosses and tombstones in order to be in an elevated position where he could see the faces of his congregation. He had the ability to hold the attention of vast audiences. On one occasion he addressed 32,000 people at the Gwennap pit. This was in part due to his remarkable voice, which Wesley himself estimated could be heard up to a distance of 140 yards.[21]

On several occasions while he was preaching disaster nearly struck, but surprisingly the members of the congregation remained just where they were, holding on to his every word. On one occasion he was speaking in Deptford, at Turner's Hall, when the floor of the building gave way, dropping several feet, but the congregation of 2,000 people remained quietly where they were and Wesley continued his address.[22] On another occasion a wall on which a great crowd was sitting collapsed, but no one cried out or changed his or her position: 'they appeared sitting at the bottom, just as they sat at the top. Nor was there any interruption either of my speaking or of the attention of the hearers.'[23]

There were other factors that resulted in Wesley's preaching being so effective. The message itself was simple and consisted of repentance, new birth, justification, the joy of salvation and the pursuit of sanctification.[24] The content of Wesley's sermons was guided by two ideas, the plain meaning of Scripture and the use of reason. Wesley was a scholar, but he was one who appealed to ordinary people; he used his scholarship to present his sermons in plain language and in an arrangement that could be both understood and remembered.

The effects of Wesley's preaching

What effect did Wesley's preaching have on those who heard him? At the heart of his preaching was his transparent sincerity, which spoke directly to the individual and appealed to the individual's conscience. One soldier recalled that when he heard Wesley preach, the great man 'turned his face towards where I stood, and I thought, fixed his eyes on me . . . and when he did speak, I thought his whole discourse was aimed at me'.[25]

But there was also a hunger for what Wesley had to say. Southey makes the point that he seldom preached to indifferent audiences. With the exception of the mobs, who were encouraged (often by the authorities) to silence him, he was listened to both by those who already believed, and by those who were merely interested and who courteously gave him their attention. Not all his hearers were poor; sometimes there were well-to-do people within his congregation or sitting in carriages on the edge of the crowd, as at Moorfields in 1739,[26] or at Bath in 1743,[27] where one wealthy man of ill-repute left half a guinea at the end of the sermon to feed and clothe the poor.

Many of those who heard Wesley preach changed their lifestyles dramatically. On Tuesday 30 September 1740 he was in London preaching on Acts 12 when a young man rushed into the congregation cursing and swearing, such that those near him wanted to march him away. But Wesley demanded that he should be allowed to stay. At the end of the sermon the young man declared that he was a smuggler on his way to work. However, he added that he would never smuggle again because he was now resolved to have the Lord for his God.[28] On another occasion, there was a sad note in Wesley's Journal concerning the unfair arrest of Edward Greenfield, a 46-year-old tinner with seven children. He was another example of someone who, three years previously, was well known for his cursing, swearing and drunkenness, but who had now turned into a good and upright citizen.[29] There are many more examples of those whose lives were changed through hearing Wesley preach. A woman who was about to end her life by throwing herself into the river passed the Foundry and heard the singing, so went inside to listen, and there found support and help. One Cornish man coming across Gulvan Downs saw a large crowd and went over to join them, and heard Wesley preach on God raising the dry bones. Twelve years later he told Wesley how that encounter had changed his life.[30]

There were many reasons for Wesley's success in preaching. His message was not only life-giving for the poor and desperate; it fitted in with changing aspirations in society. Wesley offered a vehicle by which steady conduct and upward mobility could be achieved. His invitation to give the whole of one's life to God carried with it a stewardship of time and money and resources, all of which contributed to changing people's lifestyles. But beyond these factors and Wesley's own personality and style of preaching, there was an important spiritual element for all, of whatever class. People's lives were changed because Wesley's message somehow rang true in the very depths of their being; they genuinely felt that their lives were being touched and changed by the power of God.

However, Wesley's open-air preaching was not invariably successful. One example was when he preached at Newcastle on the Town Moor to a combined force of English and German soldiers. All the soldiers were quiet and respectful, but at the end of the sermon Wesley had the distinct feeling that he had not touched their hearts.[31] It was these apparent failures that caused him to set down a strategy of where and when he would preach. He consequently decided that he would only preach in situations where he could follow the preaching with subsequent visits: 'I determin [sic] by the grace of God, not to strike one stroke in any place where I cannot follow the blow.'[32]

His preaching did result in some sensational effects, in that some of his hearers fell over, or collapsed. In his description of Wesley's field preaching, Rigg maintained that the crowds who listened sometimes gave the appearance of a routed army, with a great number of men and women falling to the ground and crying for mercy.[33] Wesley recorded in his Journal that on one occasion, when preaching on 12 June 1742 in Lincolnshire, several people dropped down as if dead and others cried and groaned, but that by the end of the service many 'lifted up their heads with joy and broke out into thanksgiving'. Preaching in London one evening, Wesley's sermon was almost inaudible because of the cries of some and the groans of others calling out to God. But in due course 'many of those who had been long in darkness saw the dawn of a great light'. He recorded that a Quaker, who stood by and looked on somewhat sceptically, himself was struck down but was restored and cried aloud that Wesley was a prophet of the Lord.[34]

One wonders if Wesley was initially surprised and worried by the effect that his preaching was having on some people. Yet he quickly justified the situation to himself by describing it as a battle for the soul of each individual:

> I can make no doubt but it was Satan tearing them, as they were coming to Christ. And hence proceeded those grievous cries, whereby he might design both to discredit the work of God, and to affright fearful people from hearing that word whereby their souls might be saved.[35]

In later life Wesley appeared keen to discourage such scenes. But it was these disorderly events that disturbed many in the Church of England and justified or strengthened their criticism of an indecent disregard for the dignity and order of the Church at these open-air events.

Wesley was not slow to defend field preaching, even though on several occasions he maintained that he would rather not do it:

> What marvel the devil does not love field-preaching! Neither do I: I love a commodious room, a soft cushion, a handsome pulpit. But where is my zeal, if I do not trample all these underfoot in order to save one more soul?[36]

He wrote an especially strong apology in 1747 addressed to those who considered it to be a vile and irreverent pursuit. His argument was that in the fields and churchyards congregations behaved, were attentive and showed a deep sense of reverence, while in St Paul's Cathedral, congregations fell asleep or talked or looked about.[37]

His defence of field preaching may have been strong, but he was also conscious that many people were genuinely disturbed by it, and it was not in his nature to cause more upset and opposition than necessary. He consequently placed field preaching as an item on the agenda of his first conference of 1744. The question was put: 'Is field preaching lawful?' The answer that Wesley penned was: 'We do not conceive that it is contrary to any law, either of God or man. Yet (to avoid any needless offence) we never preach without doors, when we can with any conveniency preach within.'[38]

Field preaching seemed far removed from the quiet scholarly life that Wesley had enjoyed in Oxford. However, he considered his ordination as a Fellow of an Oxford College did not limit him to preaching in only one parish, but gave him the freedom to preach wherever he felt called. With this interpretation he was able to travel and preach the length and breadth of the country.

The effects of Wesley's preaching are incalculable, but were never more beautifully described than by George Eliot in *Adam Bede*. Although she was writing in the middle of the nineteenth century, she was looking back to 1799 when the after-glow of Wesley's preaching was still felt:

> And this blessed gift of venerating love has been given to too many humble craftsmen since the world began, for us to feel any surprise that it should have existed in the soul of a Methodist carpenter half a century ago, while there was yet a lingering after-glow from the time when Wesley and his fellow-labourer fed on the hips and haws of the Cornwall hedges, after exhausting limbs and lungs in carrying a divine message to the poor.

She referred back to a time when Wesley's preaching was set in an amphitheatre of green hills or against a background of broad-leaved sycamore trees:

> . . . where a crowd of rough men and weary-hearted women drank in a faith which was a rudimentary culture, which linked their thoughts with the past, lifted their imagination above the sordid details of their own narrow lives, and suffused their souls with the sense of a pitying, loving, infinite Presence, sweet as summer to the houseless needy.[39]

Chapter 11

Opposition and Riots

The opposition to Methodists in the early years was widespread. It took the form of clerical opposition, from the high and powerful dignitaries of the Church to the ordinary clergy, who resented the disruption that Methodist preachers brought to their parishes. In a more violent and debased form, it produced angry mobs, often influenced by drink and encouraged by the authorities, who attacked the preachers physically and tried to drive them away by force.

Opposition to Methodism from Edmund Gibson

The most important episcopal opponent in the 1730s and 1740s was Edmund Gibson, the Bishop of London. It was his opposition that aroused a great deal of clerical hostility towards Methodism. Gibson had ordained Charles priest in 1735, and was in fact well disposed towards both brothers. He treated them kindly when they called upon him on Friday 20 October 1738. But Gibson was unhappy with the Wesleys practising any form of re-baptism of adult Dissenters, and was non-committal on the legality of religious societies meeting in private houses; nevertheless, they parted on good terms, with the Bishop assuring the brothers that they could have free access to him at any time.[1] A few months later, in February of the following year, they called on him, and he denied that he had in any way condemned them.[2] A month later, on 24 March, John and Charles again called upon the Bishop – although there is no indication at this stage that their relationship was anything but cordial. Indeed, according to Wesley, it was at a meeting with the Bishop in 1740 that he was encouraged to write and publish his *Plain Account of Christian Perfection*.[3]

However, by May 1742, Wesley, accompanied by Whitefield, was no longer given access to the Bishop, who appeared unwilling to see him on at least two occasions. A severe attack against Methodism, entitled *Observations upon the Conduct and Behaviour of a Certain Sect usually distinguished by the name of Methodists*, was published anonymously in 1744; this criticized Methodists for their excessive enthusiasm. Many people, including Wesley, suspected that this was the work of Bishop Gibson himself, a suspicion that was confirmed when the Bishop arranged for the publication to be distributed to many parts of England. A major thrust of this publication was that Methodist Societies were illegal as they were neither registered as Dissenters, nor properly belonged to the Church of England.[4] They were conventicles, and thus forbidden by law.

Gibson's 1744 publication had been preceded by Wesley's *Earnest Appeal to Men of Reason and Religion* (1743). It argued that Methodists were not (as was widely supposed) undermining the Church of England, but that they were, under the influence of their religious beliefs, leading good and holy lives. By so doing, he argued, they were 'preaching (and consequently hearing) the true word of God'; and by taking the sacrament in their parish churches they were supporting the Church rather than seeking to destroy it.[5]

Wesley was urged by a Conference of his fellow ministers and preachers in 1744 (the first of his annual 'Conferences') to write *A Farther Appeal to Men of Reason and Religion* as an additional defence of Methodism to that he had already given in his *Earnest Appeal to Men of Reason and Religion*. In section III of the *Farther Appeal* Wesley strongly maintained that Methodism was free from heresy and vice.[6] He declared that in their dedication to the work of God Methodists had suffered greater persecution than those practising 'Popery, infidelity or heresy'. He condemned the terrible riots of 1744 in the English Midlands against Methodists and asserted that his followers had not provoked the clergy: 'We have not willingly provoked them at any time; neither any single clergyman.' On the contrary, he and his followers were actually holding back from attacking the clergy: 'We have not sought occasion to publish their faults; we have not used a thousand occasions offered.'[7]

By 1747 the relationship between Gibson and Wesley had completely broken down, with the Bishop seeing Wesley as a danger to the Church, and one who must be opposed by all possible means. In his last pastoral letter to the clergy of London he wrote: 'Reverend Brothers, I charge you all lift up your voice like a trumpet! And warn, and arm and fortify all mankind against a people called Methodists.'[8]

Wesley, with genuine Christian charity, did not declare war, but wrote a reply refuting allegations against the Methodists, and appealing to the great cause of the work of God that both men shared. In the letter dated 11 June 1747, having corrected many of the misapprehensions that the Bishop held of Methodism and its beliefs, Wesley asked: 'Could your Lordship discern no other enemies of the gospel of Christ? Are there no other heretics or schismatics on earth . . . Have the Methodists (so called) already monopolized all the sins, as well as errors, in the nation? Is Methodism the only sin . . .?'[9] Wesley then went on to point out the results of his preaching, and the account he gave was said to have moved the Bishop to re-think his position.[10] Wesley wrote:

> By the fruits shall you know those of whom I speak . . . the habitual drunk-
> ard that was, is now temperate in all things; the whoremonger now flees

fornication; he that stole, steals no more, but works with his hands; he that cursed or swore, perhaps at every sentence, has now learned to serve the Lord with fear, and rejoice unto him with reverence; those formerly enslaved to various habits of sin are now brought to uniform habits of holiness. These are demonstrable facts; I can name the men, with their places of abode.[11]

He concluded his appeal, written in simple but beautiful prose, reminding the Bishop how quickly life is over and how soon all will be before the throne of God on judgement day:

My Lord, the time is short. I am past the noon of my life, and my remaining years flee away as a shadow. Your Lordship is old and full of days, having past the usual age of man. It cannot, therefore, be long before we shall drop this house of earth and stand naked before God: No, nor before we see the great white throne coming down from heaven, and Him that sitteth thereon.[12]

The Bishop made no more attacks on Methodism and died in the following year. But his earlier calls to his clergy to take up arms would have encouraged others both within and outside his diocese to oppose Wesley.

Other opponents, and rioting

Other bishops also opposed Methodism. Bishop William Warburton, of Gloucester, misunderstood Wesley and attempted to refute him by maintaining that the Holy Spirit was limited solely to the time of Jesus and the Apostles. Bishop George Lavington of Exeter was another who failed to grasp the essential mission and message of the early Methodists and described them as being Papists in disguise.[13] Opposition from members of the Church of England, combined with the fact that the early Methodists were unknown and unwelcome visitors to many districts, contributed to the riots that Wesley had to face. But these factors alone, even when seen in the context of a general pattern of eighteenth-century rioting on numerous occasions, do not fully explain the hostile opposition to the Methodists. This opposition all too quickly turned into physical violence and brutality.

During the 1740s the hardships that Wesley had endured in his travels paled into insignificance compared to the ferocity of the persecutions he faced at the hands of the mob. There were many reasons for this. The most important was that in its early days Methodism was a clerical movement within the Church of England. Initially, most of the key people, like John and Charles Wesley, were Anglican clergymen: John Fletcher, Thomas Coke, Vincent Perronet, George Whitefield, John Berridge, William Grimshaw, Henry Piers, and John Meriton.

Had they been Dissenters, local populations would have known better how to categorize them and deal with them. But being fiery young preachers of the Church of England, with strange accents who, like the friars of the Middle Ages, crossed parish boundaries at will, they raised suspicion and hostility. Even the evangelical clergy, who might have been thought of as sympathetic to Wesley, sometimes opposed him. This is partly explained by the fact that their points of reference were different from his. Wesley's inspiration came from the Early Church, whereas the evangelicals traced their point of origin back to the Reformation of the sixteenth century. Moreover, they tended to be Calvinist while he was anti-Calvinist.

Wesley's churchmanship also caused them offence. He was too High Church for the Evangelicals in his emphasis on the celebration of the sacraments and in his use of formal prayers, to which they were generally indifferent, and he was too Low Church in his disregard for church order and his invasion of the parishes of other clergy. Wesley's churchmanship led him into conflict with evangelical clergymen such as Samuel Walker, the Vicar of Truro, Henry Venn of Huddersfield, and Thomas Adams of North Lincolnshire. Clergymen such as these in the eighteenth century were not generally atheists who neglected their parishioners – many were simply quiet ministers trying to do good in sleepy parishes. However, they greatly resented the disturbance caused by Wesley and his followers, who disrupted their work and unsettled their communities.

The whole cause of the riots cannot be laid at the door of disgruntled clergy, though, or ascribed to the advent of outsiders who were neither known nor understood by the local populations. A further reason was political. The Methodist cause was not helped by rumours that the Wesleys were friends of the Pretender, or were Papist, or indeed Jesuits in disguise. The general concern about the danger of rebellion by Jacobites and a distrust of Roman Catholics (who were blamed, for example, for starting the Fire of London) was used to increase hostility towards the Methodists, by suggesting that they were in league with those who opposed the Hanoverian settlement and religious toleration.

Some of the young Methodist preachers upset their opponents by punching back when attacked. They courted opposition by preaching outside the door of the parish church, and sometimes exaggerated the ferocity of attacks on them. Wesley strongly advised his preachers not to talk about the persecution they faced, but to keep to the message of the love of God: 'instead of the wickedness of men, you might be talking of the goodness of God'.[14] But the antagonism was real. On one occasion a member of the congregation fired a gun at the preacher, and at Barnard Castle, in County Durham, the local fire engines were brought out (presumably with the knowledge and encouragement of the local authorities) to spray cold water on preacher and congregation alike.

Whitefield and Wesley must also bear some responsibility for inciting opposition to their work. Whitefield caused anger among many clergymen by attacking two well-known and much-liked devotional works. The first was *The Whole Duty of Man*, published anonymously in 1658 and highly thought of as a guide to conduct. The second was John Tillotson's *Sermons*. Tillotson (1630–94) was a loved and respected figure in the second half of the seventeenth century, who became Archbishop of Canterbury. Whitefield attacked what he considered to be Tillotson's emphasis on the moral aspects of Christianity at the expense of faith. Both Tillotson's *Sermons* and *The Whole Duty of Man* were still highly valued well into the eighteenth century; Whitefield's attack angered many High Churchmen and caused much hostility towards the Methodists, even though Wesley later included both works in his 'Christian Library'. Whitefield created yet more problems for Methodism by his thoughtless remark, widely reported, that Tillotson 'knew no more of Christ than did Mahomet'. This comment, quite obviously offensive to church people, may in fact have originated as a throwaway remark of John Wesley.[15] Certainly both men came to regret it deeply.

Violence towards Wesley and other Methodist preachers

The persecutions that the first Methodists faced were so violent that several preachers were badly injured, and those who did not have the charisma to hold the attention of a rowdy crowd were particularly susceptible to violence. William Seward, who had been introduced to Methodism through Charles Wesley and became a close friend of George Whitefield, was especially vulnerable. He had supported Methodism financially and helped in building the New Room at Bristol, as well as assisting Whitefield on his American journey. He was keen to be in the forefront of evangelism and, on accompanying Howell Harris during a Welsh preaching tour, he was blinded from stones thrown by an unruly crowd at Caerleon, near Newport. Later, while preaching at Hay-on-Wye, he was again stoned by a mob and knocked unconscious with a severe wound to the head, from which he later died.

Wesley was much better prepared to face the mob than Seward. He was brave, alert, calm under fire, and understood the psychology of crowd control. He also had a voice that compelled ordinary people to listen when he spoke. In the persecutions he faced, Wesley was at his most courageous. In certain cities, he and his fellow preachers had their rights safeguarded by the magistrates, who were influenced in their favour by the government or even by the King. Arnold Lunn told of a Quaker, who had been at Oxford with the Wesleys and later became a confidant of George II, who spoke warmly of the Wesleys to the King and assured him that they were loyal subjects.[16] The King, who disliked persecution, ensured that the magistrates in London and Bristol offered the full protection of the law. Away from these centres of population, the safety of Methodists depended much more upon the calibre of individual magistrates than upon government or royal intervention.

The Methodists suffered most from persecution in Yorkshire, Cornwall, Durham and Staffordshire, and it was in Staffordshire, on 20 October 1743,[17] that Wesley had a major confrontation with a mob from Wednesbury. He was staying at the home of Francis Ward when suddenly the house was surrounded by an angry crowd. The gathering soon dispersed, only to reassemble in greater numbers about five o'clock in the afternoon. The crowd roared 'Bring out the minister. We want the minister.' Wesley requested that the captain of the mob be brought into the house, and after a moment's conversation he changed from being a 'lion to a lamb'. Wesley repeated the process with several of the subordinate leaders, and eventually the mob settled for taking him to the magistrate, a Mr Lane. This gentleman was in bed and refused to get up, so the crowd decided to take Wesley to a Mr Persehouse, the Justice of the Peace at Walsall. However, when confronted by a rough and unruly mob from Walsall, the Wednesbury crowd ran off, leaving Wesley at the mercy of the Walsall mob.

The Walsall mob manhandled Wesley through the main street of the town with such a dreadful noise that it was impossible for him to speak except to those nearby. When Wesley attempted to seek shelter in a doorway, he was pulled back by the hair and again prevented from seeking refuge in a shop by the owner, who feared that his premises would be destroyed. Wesley stood in the doorway and asked if they would like to hear him speak. 'No, no! knock his brain out; down with him; kill him at once,' was the angry refrain. However, he *was* able to address the mob, and although he lost his voice for a short time, he continued to speak until the leader of the gang turned to him and said, 'Sir, I will spend my life for you; follow me, and not one soul here shall touch a hair of your head.' Four others quickly joined in, and with some difficulty they were able to escort Wesley out of Walsall to the open fields, from where he was able to escape back to Wednesbury. He suffered no greater injury than a grazed hand and a torn waistcoat.[18]

For five hours he had been at the mercy of a huge, angry crowd who were intent on severely beating him up, or even killing him. Yet he had survived with a strategy he was to use again and again. This involved being brave, looking the mob in the eye, and at no point attempting to run away or hide. Throughout his long ordeal he kept talking either to the individual leaders or to the mob as a whole, and he always addressed his adversaries with great courtesy and respect. When he was able to address the whole gathering, he would ask what evil he had done or which of them he had wronged in word or deed. His whole effort was to win over the leaders to his cause, knowing that they would either carry the others with them or would be strong enough to withstand the crowd.

When, in July 1745, a Cornish mob surrounded the house where he was staying at Falmouth, he used similar tactics. When his hosts fled the house he refused to hide, and when the inner door was broken down he stepped out into the roaring crowd and said:

'Here I am. Which of you has anything to say to me? To which of you have I done anything wrong? To you? or you? or you?' I continued speaking till

I came bare-headed as I was (for I purposely left my hat that they might all see my face), into the middle of the street, and then I raised my voice, said, 'Neighbours, countrymen! Do you desire to hear me speak?' They cried vehemently, 'Yes, yes. He shall speak. He shall. Nobody shall hinder him.'[19]

In his Journal, when referring to this occasion, he added a telling footnote, which said much about his whole approach to danger: 'I never saw before, no, not at Walsall itself the hand of God so plainly shown as here.'[20]

Opposition and riots continued throughout the decade. One of the worst was that orchestrated by the Reverend George White, the curate of Colne in West Yorkshire. In the summer of 1748, he preached against Wesley and raised a large, rioting mob by canvassing the local population. White had even managed to enlist James Hargrave, the constable of Barrowford, and his deputy to work in league with him. Thus, while Wesley and William Grimshaw, the Vicar of Haworth, were preaching at Roughlee, a huge mob from Colne descended upon them. One man punched Wesley in the face, and another threw his stick at him. Wesley and Grimshaw were taken off by the mob to Barrowford, where they were dragged into a house and interrogated. They were required to promise never to preach in the area again. Wesley refused to do this but, always a practical man, he compromised by saying he would not preach there again that day. The friends who accompanied him were ill-treated by the mob. They were beaten, thrown in the river, and had their hair pulled, but they and he eventually were released. On this occasion, Wesley sought legal advice from William Glanville of Gray's Inn, and Sir Dudley Ryder, the Attorney General. He then wrote to the constable of Barrowford giving a detailed account of the riots, and warning him that if he did not promise to carry out his statutory duties, Wesley would consider bringing a legal case against him.[21]

Not all the accounts of opposition given in Wesley's Journal were as serious as this or as life-threatening. Some were even humorous, such as the incident with the fair-minded magistrate of Crowle, a Mr Stovin. Wesley related that a mob arrested a cartload of 'heretics' and took them to Mr Stovin's home. When the magistrate enquired what wrong they had done, there was silence:

At length one said, 'Why they pretended to be better than other people; and besides they prayed from morning to night.' Mr Stovin asked, 'But have they done nothing besides?' 'Yes sir', said an old man: 'an't please your worship, they have *convarted* [sic] my wife. Till she went among them she had such a tongue! And now she is as quiet as a lamb.' 'Carry them back, carry them back,' replied the Justice, 'and let them convert all the scolds in the town.'[22]

It is difficult to vouch for the truth of this story; Wesley admitted that it came to him secondhand. There is, however, no doubt that Mr Stovin was a good example of a magistrate who was friendly and sympathetic, and even permitted Wesley on a return journey to Crowle to preach in his garden.

Gradually, as Wesley became more and more part of the English scene and people got used to him, persecution and opposition died down. Churches were once more open to him, bishops befriended him, and clergy travelled many miles to hear him preach, while local clergy, who came to know him personally, were keen to administer Holy Communion alongside him. He outlived the enmity against him and, as an old man, the crowds who had once mobbed him lined the streets to cheer him and flocked to hear him preach. The Methodists had, by dint of courage, tenacity and perseverance, come to be accepted for what they were – a force for good in eighteenth-century Britain. That achievement was not gained without struggle, year after year; and the whole heroic process gives a wonderful resonance, even a literal meaning, to Charles Wesley's hymn of 1749: 'And are we yet alive/And see each other's face?' In 1749 it must have seemed like an annual miracle that these preachers were still alive:

What troubles have we seen!
What conflicts have we passed!
Fightings without, and fears within
Since we assembled last.

But out of all the Lord
Hath brought us by his love . . .

In John Wesley's lifetime, and ever since, this hymn has been used to open the Methodist Conference. Its delegates today would do well to remember, as they sing these verses, the bravery, the endurance and the dedication of those who faced ridicule and danger in those early years.

Chapter 12

The Travelling Preacher

John Wesley, although small in stature, had enormous stamina. Few people in the history of the Church have matched his extraordinary capacity for work. Even St Paul's missionary journeys seem short when compared with Wesley's preaching journeys of over fifty years around the United Kingdom. He travelled some 250,000 miles, much of it on poor roads and tracks. In 1741, with the exception of a few miles of road at Whitehaven, there were no turnpike roads north of the Humber, and it was left to local parishes to maintain the roads that ran through their boundaries. By 1770 a good network of turnpike roads had been developed, linking the main centres of population. However, off the main roads, in the Dales, the North Yorkshire Moors, and Lancashire hills, where Wesley was still travelling in old age, many of the roads were considered to be unpassable by a horse and trap. On 23 May 1781, aged 77, he wrote in his Journal: 'Having appointed to preach at Blackburn I was desired to take Kabb in my way. But such a road sure no carriage ever went before; I was glad to quit it and use my own feet.'

Wesley estimated that he never travelled less than 4,500 miles a year. Throughout his life he followed the strict regime of rising at 4 a.m., preaching at 5 a.m., and travelling some sixty miles a day to preach at two or three more places before evening. During these long days of travelling, on horseback with a loose rein, he would read books, write letters or prepare sermons. While riding from Norwich to Yarmouth in 1765, for example, he read Isaac Watts's *The Improvement of the Mind*, and by the end of his journey had produced a good critical account of the book.[1] He often used the journey time to produce abridged versions of devotional works for his 'Christian Library'.

The strategy behind Wesley's travels

What was Wesley's strategy behind all his activities of travelling and preaching? There is a widespread misapprehension that Wesley travelled to every place in the United Kingdom and founded a Society in every town and village. There were, however, large areas of the country where Methodism was practically unknown. Moreover, Wesley was not always travelling round the country. In the dark winter months he tended to base his activities in London or Bristol, even though in December and January he would undertake shorter regional journeys, travelling as far afield as Canterbury or Birmingham. Once spring was on the way he would set out to the north of England or Wales, Ireland or Cornwall. In the early years of his travelling, his plan was not to cover the whole country but instead to concentrate his preaching on large centres of population, especially London, Bristol and Newcastle. In these cities the population was less dominated by a restrictive parish system, and the people were generally more free to follow Wesley's leadership. He seems to have had little interest in the fashionable resorts; nor did he visit regularly areas whose economy was solely based on agriculture. The hierarchical pattern of the squire and vicar, together with the tenant farmers and agricultural labourers, was a difficult society to break into. So was the agricultural society in which workers were dependent on being hired by the farmers, even when, as in North Lincolnshire, which he continued to visit after his father's death, the agricultural activity was supplemented by an industry that made sacking from flax at Epworth, and by fishing at Grimsby.

Wesley's approach to evangelism was not like that of Whitefield, who preached to vast congregations and then moved on, hoping that, having sowed the seed, others would come and reap the harvest. Wesley's strategy was one of concentration on various centres and groups of people. His Journal clearly shows that in the first ten years as a travelling preacher he concentrated on London, Bristol and Newcastle, where he began to expand his work westwards into Tynedale and southwards into Weardale and Teesdale and gradually down to the Leeds area. It was not long before he was extending his work into Cornwall and Staffordshire. However, there were particular groups of workers with whom he made great headway, and on which he naturally concentrated his efforts. These included the tinners of Cornwall, the miners and keelmen of Durham and Newcastle, the lead miners of Weardale, and the fishermen from towns along the east coast of England.

The heart of Wesley's message

What was the message that Wesley was so keen to preach on these journeys, and indeed what was the reason and purpose behind all his travelling? It is difficult to extract in a succinct form the essence of what he was trying to communicate to his hearers from his many published sermons; these were only a fraction of the 40,000 sermons he preached during his lifetime. Fortunately, though, Wesley himself expressed the heart of his message in a conversation in 1745 with a wealthy man who had fallen upon hard times and tried to take his own life.[2] The man had asked Wesley what was the aim and purpose of his preaching. Wesley replied that it was to make people virtuous and happy, at ease with themselves, and useful to others. Moreover, he wished to lead those who would listen 'to heaven and to God, the Judge and lover of all and to Jesus, the Mediator of the new covenant'.[3] Wesley went on to explain that he preached a religion of love and the law of kindness as shown in the Gospels. It was his hope that his hearers would come to enjoy God and themselves and to conquer the fear of death. According to Wesley, it was also the duty of all Christians to love their neighbours, and comfort those who were miserable. This message was probably more effective because Wesley delivered it in person and thereby ensured that it was accompanied by his evident kindness and goodwill; he was generous and friendly in demeanour, which helped to attract and convince people.

The dangers for travelling preachers

Life as a travelling preacher in the eighteenth century was difficult and dangerous. Wesley not only had to contend with poor roads and tracks with few signposts, but he also had to put up with atrocious weather, poor accommodation, hostility and highwaymen. At the end of his *Farther Appeal to Men of Reason and Religion* (1745) he came to the conclusion that only someone who was genuinely called by God could put up with all the hardship that this work involved, and asked:

> Can you bear the summer sun to beat upon your naked head? Can you suffer the wintry rain or wind, from whatever quarter it blows? Are you able to stand in the open air without any covering or defence when God casteth abroad his snow like wool, or scatter his hoar-frost like ashes? And yet these are some of the smallest inconveniences.[4]

There were yet other hazards. Although Wesley was an accomplished horseman, there were several occasions when he got into difficulty. He was riding through Borough a few days before Christmas 1765 when his horse fell and trapped Wesley's leg underneath it. A shopkeeper came to his aid and took him in and gave him a drink; Wesley was very sick, badly bruised and unable to walk, so he had to get a carriage back home. Over the next few weeks he tried desperately to carry out his preaching commitments, but a week after the accident he was too poorly to preach at West Street Chapel and had to ask Mr Greaves to stand in for him.[5]

Bad weather was an inherent difficulty faced by Wesley in his field preaching. In March 1779 he was just commencing his sermon at Bromwich Heath when he and his congregation were engulfed in a spectacular hailstorm. As there was no building large enough to contain the gathering, he continued to preach in the open air but was all the time fearful that tiles would come crashing down from the surrounding houses.[6] On another occasion, in February 1745, while heading north from Doncaster, Wesley rode into a terrible snowstorm. There was so much snow that progress was very slow and darkness fell while he and his companions still had six miles to go to their evening's lodgings. However, they pushed on across the moor, and by about 8 p.m. came safely to Sandhutton.[7] Worse was to come, and by the next morning the snow was so deep that many places were impassable. The ice had thawed and then frozen again, turning the countryside into a sheet of glass. It was impossible for the party to ride their horses, and even while being led, the horses constantly slipped and fell. Progress was painfully slow and, again, night had fallen long before they reached Gateshead Fell, which in the deep snow appeared as a vast pathless waste.[8] Fortunately, a local man who knew the way overtook them and guided them safely into Newcastle. Wesley commented in his Journal: 'Many a rough journey have I had before, but one like this I never had; between wind, and hail, and rain, and ice, and snow, and driving sleet, and piercing cold.'[9]

Crossing the sea could be a dangerous venture in poor weather, and the Irish Sea, which Wesley crossed 42 times, could be notoriously rough. On Friday 2 August 1765, Wesley found that the captain of the *Felicity*, with whom he had arranged his passage back to England, had set off without him, even though Wesley's horse was on board. On learning that the *Felicity* was anchored a few miles out at sea, Wesley took a small boat and was able to catch up with the ship before it sailed to Whitehaven. Because of contrary winds, the crossing took four days.

One of the difficulties that Wesley created for himself was that he often made his plans several weeks in advance and announced well ahead the time and the location where he would be preaching. In order not to disappoint his would-be hearers, he was often compelled to travel at great speed, whatever the weather or the conditions of the roads or ferries. Sometimes he took more risks than he might have done in other circumstances. On Monday 24 October 1743 he set out from Epworth for Grimsby, but on reaching the River Trent at Owston Ferry, the boatmen would not attempt the crossing because of a storm. The Trent north of Gainsborough has always been a wide and dangerous stretch of river, in which over the years many people have lost their lives owing to its whirlpools and fast-flowing tidal currents. Wesley waited an hour, but was unwilling to disappoint the congregation at Grimsby and persuaded the boatmen to set out against their better judgement. His account of the crossing is vivid, and even – at the end – humorous:

Many stood looking after on the river-side in the middle of which we were, when, in an instant, the side of the boat was under water, and the horses and men rolling one over another. We expected the boat to sink every moment; but I did not doubt of being able to swim ashore. The boatmen were amazed, as well as the rest; but they quickly recovered, and rowed for life. And soon after, our horses leaping overboard lightened the boat, and we all came unhurt to land.

They wondered what was the matter. I did not rise (for I lay along in the bottom of the boat); and I wondered too, till, upon examination, I found that a large iron crow, which the boatmen sometimes used, was (none knew how) run through the string of my boot, which pinned me down that I could not stir; so that if the boat had sunk, I should have been safe enough from swimming any farther.[10]

The Trent continued to cause Wesley trouble. Twenty years later, it had flooded at Misterton and the following day he was unable to take the ferry at Althorpe because of the strong winds, so rather than delay and be late for his appointment in Hull he rode further up the river to make the crossing.[11]

In the summer of the same year, 1764, Wesley set out from Shrewsbury at 4 a.m. to ride through Wales to Pembroke. It was a horrendous journey during which he was misdirected, ending up on the edge of a peat bog, lost on a mountainside, and misled by a drunken miner, who sobered up after he had fallen into a stream. Eventually, at midnight, having been travelling for 24 hours, Wesley and his companion came to a remote inn, but there was no hay for the horses. However, they were each found somewhere to sleep. Early the next morning Wesley was horrified to find that the drunken miner and the ostler had been out all night riding their horses. Both animals had been ill-treated and were bleeding from wounds they had received. Wesley then remembered that he had a letter from a Nathaniel Williams and, upon enquiry, found that he lived only a mile away from the inn. Wesley and his companion walked to the house of Mr Williams, where both men and animals were well received. After resting for a while, he preached to the family and friends, and then set off in the early afternoon for Lampeter. Here he wrote an important letter to Lord Dartmouth on a proposal for union among the clergy.[12] The next day he rode through Carmarthen and on to Pembroke.[13]

Wesley's powers of endurance as a travelling preacher

Wesley's powers of endurance were remarkable. He continued to travel through the United Kingdom on horseback until he was 70 years old. He then took to riding in a small carriage or a horse and trap. Even with a different type of transport, he kept up a similar regime of travelling. He was, by then, assisted by a much improved network of turnpike roads, which by 1770 covered most areas of the country. He probably paid more in tolls than any other person in England, although it is not surprising to note that this integrated road system, which helped him so much in his travelling, was a development that he himself opposed on the grounds that the tolls would prevent poor people from travelling.[14] He commended those who had worked hard to improve the Thirsk to

Stokesley road, which used to be of a poor quality, but by 1770 this was better than most turnpike roads: it was exceptional in that all could travel along free of charge, 'without saddling the poor people with the vile imposition of turnpikes for ever'.[15]

In 1777 he visited the Isle of Man at the age of 73, and in Castletown he estimated that the entire population had turned out to hear him preach.[16] He was greatly impressed by the inhabitants of the island: 'A more loving, simple-hearted people than this I never saw . . . It is supposed to contain nearly thirty thousand people, remarkably courteous and humane.'[17]

But even here Wesley was not free of danger in his travels. While driving a one-horse chaise with Mrs Smyth as his passenger, a wheel caught against a large stone and the chaise overturned, but 'we fell so gently on smooth grass that neither of us was hurt at all.'[18] Wesley went on to preach to a large congregation that evening in Douglas. Also, when he was well over 80, Wesley visited the Channel Isles (in 1787) and was pleased to find that in Jersey his preaching was still well received.

As an older man, Wesley seemed less concerned about danger than before. In the summer of 1774 he set out from Newcastle to Horsley with Mr Hooper and Mr Smith. He took Mrs Smith and her two young daughters in the chaise with him. Two miles from Horsley the horses suddenly bolted and shot down the hill with such speed that the coachman was flung off the box. The chaise came dangerously near the ditch at one side and then on the other. The horses avoided a cart coming towards them, and miraculously managed to squeeze through a narrow bridge, then through a gate, across a farmyard and on through a corn-field, after having broken down a second gate:

> The little girls cried out, 'Grandpapa save us!' I told them, 'Nothing will hurt you: do not be afraid'; feeling no more fear or care (blessed be God!) than if I had been sitting in my study. The horses ran on till they came to the edge of a steep precipice. Just then Mr Smith, who could not overtake us before, galloped in between. They stopped in a moment. Had they gone ever so little, he and we must have gone down together.[19]

The perils of the traveller in the eighteenth century were not limited to poor roads, dangerous ferries and runaway horses; there was also the threat of highwaymen. In the afternoon of 13 August 1782 Wesley, who was then in his eightieth year, left London by coach for Bristol. Not long after midnight the coach party was informed that there were highwaymen on the road ahead who had robbed every passing coach. Wesley wrote, 'I felt no uneasiness on the account, knowing that God would take care of us.'[20]

When he was 87 he was still preaching in Yorkshire, Lincolnshire and Norfolk. On the evening of 13 October he preached at Norwich, and the congregation – once again – could not be contained in the building. Wesley commented, 'How wonderfully is the tide turned! I am become an honourable man at Norwich. God has at length made our enemies to be at peace with us.'[21] As the years went by, he became more and more accepted and beloved; his visits were welcomed like those of an old and dear friend.

Old age did not prevent him from travelling to Newcastle, Cornwall or Ireland, all of which seemed to have a special place in his affections. He also had a natural affinity with the Irish and enjoyed great success there. Methodism was the only Protestant branch of Christianity to make much progress in Ireland in the eighteenth century, and in Dublin Wesley had his largest following outside London. The account of his departure from Ireland for the last time, 18 months before his death, is a good indication of the affection and esteem in which he was held. It was related by a Mr Stopford:

> Multitudes followed him down to the ship. Time had done its work; 'the keepers of the house trembled, and the strong man bowed himself.' Wesley was then eighty-seven years old. Before he went on board the vessel he gave out a hymn, and they sang. He then kneeled with the multitudes upon the ground, and offered a fervent prayer for those who were present, for their families, and for God's blessing upon the Church, and especially upon Ireland. He then shook hands with them. Many wept, and a number fell upon his neck and kissed him. The scene was tenderly impressive. After Mr Wesley went on board the ship he stood upon the deck with uplifted hands blessing them, while those on the shore waved their handkerchiefs till the winds of heaven wafted him out of their sight, and they beheld him no more.[22]

Wesley was a cheerful traveller who made the best of every situation. According to Alexander Knox:

> His countenance, as well as conversation, expressed an habitual gaiety of heart, which nothing but conscious virtue and innocence could have bestowed. He was, in truth, the most perfect specimen of moral happiness which I ever saw.[23]

He was a good companion and was never more satisfied than when travelling in the company of happy people. Arnold Lunn quotes him as saying, 'I am content with what ever entertainment I meet with and my companions are always in good humour. This must be the spirit of all who take journeys with me.'[24]

His enjoyment of travel and people

Wesley was a child of his age in the sense that he took great delight in the scenery of the countryside as he passed through. For example, in 1779 he went out of his way to visit the gardens at Stowe,[25] which he found very pleasing, though not as much as he had enjoyed the gardens at Stourhead. He particularly commended the beautiful situation at Stourhead, noting that 'all the gardens hang on the sides of a semicircular mountain'.[26] He delighted in the Irish towns, especially Doneraile, which he considered to be one of the most pleasant towns in the kingdom. He commented on the small things of life that brought happiness, like a pleasant wind on a hot day while riding into Dublin.[27] After his long and arduous journey over the Welsh mountains he observed, 'We rode through a lovely vale, and over pleasant and fruitful hills to Carmarthen.'[28] One of the factors that makes Wesley's Journal so attractive to read is that it records the journey of a happy and contented traveller, as well as the efforts of a dedicated and determined man.

Finally, we must not forget the hospitality given to Wesley, which was a vital part of his itinerant ministry. Wesley had three homes he could use: in London at the Foundry, and later at City Road; at Bristol; and at the Orphan House in Newcastle. He enjoyed being able to spend some time in each of them reading and writing, but most of all he enjoyed spending time in the homes of good friends. There were hundreds of men and women who took him into their homes, gave him meals, found him a bed, and restored and refreshed him before sending him on his journey. In this way there grew up a great tradition of Methodist hospitality. Wesley's friends provided for him something more than an eighteenth-century Travelodge where he could break his journey and spend the night; they gave him kindness and care, hospitality and friendship, which empowered him on his travels. A letter he received from Mrs Sally Nind of Romsbury Park, the wife of a prosperous farmer, was typical of many warm invitations:

> If dear Mr Wesley has any time for retirement this winter, we shall be exceeding glad if he will please to come to Romsbury Park, where we shall think it an honour to furnish him, as the Shunamite did the Prophet Elisha, with a bed, a stool and a candlestick.[29]

In his turn, Wesley preached in their homes, read the Bible, said prayers, and blessed them. He left behind a deep feeling of goodness and compassion, and a sense that they belonged to God, were valued by him, and were living in his presence. In this way Wesley built up a vast network of Christian friendship and hospitality, which was unique in the history of the Church. In describing Wesley's last visit to Dublin, Crookshank captured well the effect that Wesley had on the people he visited: 'They seemed to think it a blessing to have him under their roof; and such a sacred influence attended his words that it was no ordinary privilege to have the opportunity of listening to his conversation.'[30]

His journeys were much more than the tours of a preacher; they were equally important as a means of building this matrix of friendship. It was the love and care of the members of the Societies for one another that was a lasting legacy of Wesley's life.

Chapter 13

Theological and Matrimonial Strife

The decade from 1748 to 1758 was a turbulent one in Wesley's life, marked by several high and low points. At the beginning of the decade he preached for the first time his remarkable sermon on the 'Catholic Spirit' to a congregation in Newcastle. The sermon was a call to put aside the many ecclesiastical differences found within the Church and, in Wesley's haunting words, which included those of his text, 'Let all these smaller points stand aside. Let them never come into sight. "If thine heart is as my heart", if thou lovest God and all mankind, I ask no more: "give me thine hand".'[1] However, his interpretation of the 'Catholic Spirit' was sadly not wide enough to include the Roman Catholic Church. Within a short period of preaching the sermon, he had published his *Roman Catechism*, in which he tried to show the unscriptural nature of the Roman Catholic Church.

In the same year, 1749, that he produced his sermon on the 'Catholic Spirit', Wesley cancelled a journey to Rotterdam in order to prepare a paper to refute Dr Conyers Middleton's *A Free Inquiry into Miraculous Powers, which are supposed to have subsisted in the Christian Church* (1748). Middleton, a Fellow of Trinity College, Cambridge, had attempted to show that there were no miracles performed either by Jesus or in the Early Church, and that the Apostolic Fathers were either foolish or naïve. This thesis struck right at the heart of Wesley's ecclesiastical system, which took the Early Church as a major point of reference. In his letter to Middleton, Wesley acknowledged that few of the Early Church Fathers had much learning; he also conceded that they had a great many failings. Nevertheless he accorded reverence to them because they were Christians and he saw few people in his own day who could match them. Moreover Wesley maintained that their writing described genuine Christianity. This long letter was one of the few occasions when Wesley took the initiative to enter into theological controversy. Another dispute that demanded Wesley's attention at this time was the Calvinistic controversy referred to in Chapter 9. Although Wesley had been engaged in the controversy for 13 years, it was not until 1752 that he produced his first anti-Calvinistic paper entitled *Predestination calmly considered*, where he argued that Christ died for all and not 'only for the elect'.

Wesley and Dr John Taylor of Norwich

One of Wesley's major confrontations of this decade was that with Dr John Taylor over the doctrine of original sin. At the time of this dispute, Taylor was the minister of the recently completed Octagon Chapel in Norwich, and shortly to become the first Principal of the Warrington Academy. He was a very successful minister and had acquired a considerable reputation as a leading biblical scholar after the publication of his Hebrew grammar. Wesley had visited the Octagon Chapel soon after its completion and admired it as one of the finest chapels in Europe.

Both Wesley and Taylor had been influenced by the writings of the ecumenically minded and eirenical Richard Baxter. Both saw the Bible as being at the centre of their respective theologies. It was Taylor's biblical studies that led him to reject the doctrine of original sin, as developed by Augustine of Hippo, believing that it was based on erroneous interpretations of the biblical texts. Wherever Taylor's ideas had taken hold, Wesley found that he could make little progress, so in 1757 he published *The Doctrine of Original Sin*, which argued that if you remove the doctrine of original sin you undermine the scriptural doctrine of Christian redemption. Orthodoxy was clearly on Wesley's side in this controversy, but Taylor had argued a good and rational case. Looking back on the confrontation 250 years later, Taylor's biographer, Geoffrey Eddy, has observed that Wesley was far too pessimistic about human nature, while Taylor was far too optimistic.

Wesley's relationship with Grace Murray

During the decade 1748–58 a far greater impact on Wesley's life than these theological confrontations was that made by two women: Grace Murray and Mary Vazeille.

From August 1748 until her marriage in October 1749, Grace Murray dominated John Wesley's life, so much so that she has been described as 'Wesley's last love'.[2] She was born in January 1716 and, at the age of 16, went to live with her sister to avoid being coerced by her parents into a marriage to a man she did not love. Shortly afterwards she went into domestic service, and at the age of 18 married a sailor, Alexander Murray. Life was not easy for her; while her husband was away at sea she had a miscarriage, and later her only child died in infancy. It was while lonely and bereaved that she heard Whitefield preaching in London and was greatly moved by his sermon. She made up her mind to hear Wesley preach at Moorfields:

> I rose at 3 & about 4 set out tho' I knew not where Moorfields was. I overtook a Woman going thither who shew'd me ye way. When Mr W(esley) stood up, & looked round on ye Congregation, I fixt my Eyes

upon him, & felt an inexpressible Conviction, that he was sent of GOD.[3]

On returning home, Grace's husband was very disappointed at her conversion. He threatened to put her in a lunatic asylum, but eventually relented and set out on another long voyage. A few months later he was drowned.

Wesley was quick to see that Grace was a woman of real dedication and ability, so he made her a band leader, a sick visitor, and later put her in charge of the Orphan House at Newcastle. This was not, as the name suggests, a home for orphans, but was his northern headquarters, which contained a preaching house, a school, a Sunday school and, later on, a medical dispensary, as well as residential accommodation. Grace later became a member of the group who, from time to time, accompanied him on his preaching journeys.

Wesley for his part had shown no interest in a romantic relationship since his disastrous entanglement with Sophia Hopkey in Georgia. However, at the age of 45, during the Conference of June 1748, Wesley became persuaded by the other preachers that 'a Believer might marry without suffering loss in his soul'.[4] The following August, while travelling in the north-east of England, he was taken ill with a series of violent headaches. Grace Murray, who was in Newcastle, nursed Wesley through this illness. It has often been pointed out that he always found himself attracted to women who were nursing him. Sophia Hopkey had nursed him in Georgia, Grace Murray nursed him in Newcastle, and Mary Vazeille, the future Mrs Wesley, was to nurse him in London. While Grace Murray was looking after him, he suddenly saw her in a new light. He wrote: 'I observ'd her more narrowly than ever before, both as to her Temper, Sense & Behaviour. I esteem'd & loved her more & more.'[5]

He subsequently told her that if ever he married she would be the person. Grace seemed amazed and replied, 'This is too great a Blessing for me: I can't tell how to believe it. This is all I cou'd have wish'd for under Heaven . . .'[6] Wesley was convinced that God had called Grace Murray to be his fellow labourer and he told her so. He explained that they must part, but promised that he would take her to Ireland with him in the following spring. She begged that she might be allowed to accompany him on his travels, so the two of them set out for Yorkshire and Derbyshire. At one point in the journey, Wesley left her in the care of John Bennet at Chester. This was Wesley's biggest mistake in the whole affair, as Grace Murray and John Bennet were already attracted to one another. It also seems to have been one of Grace Murray's weaknesses that she found herself most attracted to the person she was with at the time.

Wesley was soon to receive two letters, one from John Bennet and one from Grace Murray, asking for his consent for them to marry each other. Grace added to her request that 'she believed that it was the will of God'.[7] Wesley was devastated but, believing that there was nothing he could do, wrote a 'mild' answer. He was surprised to get such an affectionate reply from Grace. The marriage did not take place and, when Grace and Wesley met again, she told him that she could not believe that Wesley's had been a real proposal of marriage. She accompanied him to Ireland, where he found her a great help in his evangelism, and in the care of the Irish Societies. They much enjoyed one another's company and, by the end of the Irish tour, Wesley had confirmed his desire to marry Grace.

He then set out in some detail the reasons for and against marrying her. In this exercise we see Wesley being rational even about love. In favour of marrying Grace, Wesley listed the fact that she would not add to his expenses, she would be a good housekeeper, she was neat and tidy, frugal, obeyed the rules, was a good nurse, would save him from being molested by other women, and would be a fellow labourer in the gospel. Against marrying her, he listed three objections, which he quickly dismissed. First, she came from a poor home, but that did not worry him. Second, she had been his servant, but that had enabled him to know her well before he married her. Third, she had travelled with him, which could lead people to say she was his mistress before she was his wife. This he dismissed on the grounds that it was not true, and in any case he was used to slander. Moreover, he asserted that he would not marry any woman who could not travel with him. He concluded that he had a better claim to Grace than John Bennet.[8]

Although this process seemed very mechanical, there is no doubt that Wesley loved Grace Murray. But, once again, Wesley was destined to be unfortunate in love. Just when everything seemed to be settled, Grace, who at this time was in Bristol, heard false rumours of Wesley's attachment to a certain Molly Francis. Feeling jilted by Wesley, she immediately wrote to John Bennet to re-establish her relationship with him. On Tuesday 29 August 1749 Bennet, Grace Murray and Wesley met at Epworth, where Wesley had a long conversation with Bennet. Although deeply in love with Grace, he decided that Bennet should marry her. However, this was not the end of the saga, as it appears that neither man had fully consulted Grace, who a few days later informed Wesley that she was determined to marry him. Wesley felt an obligation to consult the Societies, seek his brother's permission, and satisfy Bennet, but he was confident that they could be married within the year. He started this process by writing to Bennet, explaining the predicament.

At this stage, Charles Wesley was alerted to the situation. He was concerned about John marrying a woman who was promised to another man, and also troubled that she had been a servant. Charles rode to meet Grace Murray at Hindley, near Newcastle, telling her that she had broken his heart. He persuaded her to ride pillion on the back of his horse and took her to John Bennet in Newcastle. She felt that she had treated John Bennet badly, and asked for his forgiveness. Within a few days Bennet and Grace Murray were married in St Andrew's Church, Newcastle. John Wesley was devastated; the same feelings that he had experienced when Sophia Hopkey married Williamson returned to him. He described his feelings, 'I was in great heaviness, my heart was sinking in me like a stone.'[9]

Luckily, Whitefield proved a true friend; he stayed with Wesley at this time and brought him great comfort, as well as playing a major part in restoring the impaired relationship between the Wesley brothers. When Wesley and Bennet met, Wesley kissed Bennet and then continued his preaching and travelling the next day. Tyerman made the following assessment of the affair: 'Wesley was a dupe; Grace Murray was a flirt; John Bennet was a cheat; Charles Wesley was a sincere, but irritated, impetuous, and officious friend.'[10]

However, it is all too easy to lay the blame on one or other of the people involved. In assessing the situation, it is important to remember that Grace Murray was seeking a stable home and family life that had been missing in her childhood and in her first marriage, where she had experienced the death of a child. John Wesley, although genuinely in love with her, was already deeply committed to the Methodist movement and, moreover, seemed to find it difficult to make up his mind about marriage until it was too late. John Bennet was obviously fond of Grace Murray, and only seems to have made moves towards marrying her when encouraged to do so. Charles Wesley, although misguided, appears to have acted from the best of motives.

John Bennet soon removed himself from Wesley's service and later joined the Calvinists. He was greatly missed, as he was not only a man with a sound education who had his own means of support, but he was also a brave and good preacher. Three days after her wedding, Wesley had a short conversation with Grace Murray, but then the two did not meet again for almost forty years, when, in 1788, Grace's son was preaching in Moorfields and she came to visit him. At her request, Wesley went to see her. He was 85 and she was 72. The meeting was cordial, although it did not last long, and was the last time the two former friends saw each other.

Marriage to Mary Vazeille

On Sunday 10 February 1751 Wesley was walking across London Bridge in the early morning when he slipped on the ice, fell, and badly hurt his ankle. Although he attempted to continue with his appointments, in the end he had to be carried back to the Foundry on a chair. He was then moved to Threadneedle Street, where he was nursed by Mrs Mary Vazeille, a widow with three children. Within a few days he had proposed marriage, she had accepted, and the two were married. Two London periodicals reported the marriage: the *Gentleman's Magazine*, which gave the date as 18 February, referring to the new Mrs Wesley as a lady with an income of some £300 per year; and the *London Magazine*, which reported the marriage as taking place on the following day.[11] It is interesting that Wesley did not refer to either his marriage or his honeymoon in his Journal, but simply left a week unaccounted for. Moreover, with this romance Wesley did not consult either his brother or the Methodist Societies; he simply went ahead with the wedding, even though earlier in the month he had spoken to the unmarried preachers 'and showed them on how many accounts it was good for those who have received that gift from God to remain "single for the kingdom of heaven's sake" '.

At first the marriage seemed happy. Mrs Wesley was an attractive woman, and the letters that passed between them were full of affection, trust and love. They contained phrases such as 'I feel you every day nearer to my heart', and 'I shall never love any creature better than I love you'.[12] In early April Wesley was writing to 'my dearest earthly friend'.[13] He also added a postscript to a letter of this time that he must have later greatly regretted, 'If any letter comes to you, directed to the Revd. Mr. John Wesley, open it – it is for yourself.'[14]

Mary made a great effort to travel with him, which cannot have been easy for her. On 6 July 1752, unable to get a boat from Deeside to Whitehaven, she rode all that day with Wesley to Manchester and on to Whitehaven, which they reached four days later. Sometimes she had to endure the mobs. At Hull, a mob attacked Wesley and his wife, but a brave woman offered them the security of her coach. The mob then attacked the coach, and threw things through the windows. Wesley seems to have been well protected as 'a large gentlewoman who sat in my lap screened me, so that nothing came near me'.[15] One wonders what happened to Mrs Wesley and whether her husband was looking after her.

For the next few years the affectionate letters continued to pass between them. Wesley kindly reassured her that she was well thought of among the Methodist Societies.[16] In 1755 we find that she again accompanied him on a journey through the north-east of England. However, by the end of the decade their marriage was in serious trouble, and there were several reasons for this.

On 31 March 1754 Mary returned to London to be at the bedside of her dying son. The death of her child must have affected her far more than Wesley seemed to realize by the note in his Journal for that day. It gave her a greater need for Wesley's time, understanding and sympathetic love. It probably caused her to be more jealous of his friendships with others, especially the large network of women friends with whom Wesley regularly corresponded.

His extensive travelling must also have placed a great strain on the marriage, for she was continually faced with the choice of braving the rigours and hardships of eighteenth-century journeys, and of being separated from her children, or being lonely at home, not quite sure where her husband was. It was a recipe for disaster; Mary became more and more bitter, jealous and angry, while her husband, although he tried hard, did not know how to deal with the situation. Wesley found Mary a place in his book room, where her organizational abilities were put to good use. But by 1757 he no longer wished his letters to go via his wife,[17] and the situation came to a head in 1758.

One of the reasons for the breakdown of the relationship between Wesley and his wife was a letter he had written to Sarah Ryan, which Mrs Wesley had found in his coat pocket.[18] In it he said, 'The conversing with you, either by speaking or writing, is an unspeakable blessing to me. I cannot think of you without thinking of God.' Wesley always wrote with great affection to men and women within the Methodist movement; indeed, it was the friendship of Wesley that held those early Societies together. Although there were no sexual overtones either stated or intended in the letters to these women within the Methodist movement, it is not difficult to see that to someone who was already feeling isolated, vulnerable and jealous, this correspondence would have aroused great anger.

In January 1758 Mary left John and vowed she would never see him again.[19] Although she later returned and there were moments of affection between them, the marriage was doomed to failure from this time onwards.

In the years that followed there was much hostility between the two of them as she came and went. He complained that she had picked his locks and stolen his papers.[20] After being married for eight years, Wesley wrote a long letter to Mary in which he set out clearly, but perhaps unwisely, the things he disliked about her. There were ten major points: (1) showing his papers to other people; (2) not allowing him to have command of his own home; (3) making him a prisoner in his own home; (4) making him a prisoner outside his own home; (5) making him not feel safe in his own house; (6) mistreating his servants; (7) talking against him; (8) slandering him; (9) saying untrue things; (10) her bitterness towards those who defended him.[21]

Wesley may have been to blame in many respects for the breakdown of the marriage, but he was never a vindictive man, and was always reluctant to give up on anyone. Even at this time, he appears to have had love and affection for Mary. In July 1760 he wrote a charming letter to her, 'if you want to make the best of a few days, to improve the evening of life, let us begin today! And what we do let us do it with our might. Yesterday is past, and not to be recalled; to-morrow is not ours. Now Molly, let us set out.'[22]

The Wesleys' turbulent marriage continued through the 1760s and 1770s. In 1766 Mary sent her good wishes via Wesley to Mr Ebenezer Blackwell[23] and in the same year Wesley noted with some pleasure that his wife continued to be in a good temper, and added 'Miracles are not ceased.'[24] Mary left home in 1769 and again in 1771, when she vowed never to return. Wesley wrote in Latin in his Journal: 'I have not left her; I have not sent her away; I will not recall her.' During this period there were moments when he wondered if she had gone mad. Charles Wesley, when writing to John at this time, somewhat cynically referred to Mrs Wesley as 'your best friend'. But there were also moments of compassion and understanding. Again, in 1772, a year after Mary had 'finally left him', the two of them were together, and Wesley referred to his wife as one 'Finding fault in nobody, but well pleased with every person and thing!'[25] That summer they travelled together and Wesley recorded that on one occasion they stayed at a small inn on the moors, where he and the innkeeper, Mary and the innkeeper's wife had a pleasant conversation.[26] Although in later years she does not often appear in his correspondence or his Journal, there is an appreciative letter that he wrote to her in 1774: 'My Dear Love, Your behaviour as to the money was admirable.

You did yourself much honour thereby. You behaved like a woman of honour, sense and conscience.'[27] His Journal entries also suggest that he still trusted her to deal with some of his financial affairs.[28]

The final break appears to have come in 1775, when Mrs Wesley left home again, taking with her some of Wesley's letters, extracts of which she showed to his Calvinistic opponents. It has been suggested that she deliberately mutilated and edited them in order to destroy Wesley's reputation.[29] It is easy to see how passages could be extracted from Wesley's letters and used to support false allegations of sexual impropriety. According to Tyerman,[30] these falsified and interlined letters with forged names were sent by Mary to the *Morning Post*. When Charles Wesley pleaded with him to refute the reports, John simply replied, 'when I devoted to God my ease, my time, my life, did I except my reputation? No. Tell Sally I will take her to Canterbury tomorrow.'[31]

Two years later, on 1 September 1777, he wrote a letter to his wife, having met her a few days previously, when she expressed a wish to return home. In this letter he laid down three conditions: (1) That she should return his papers. (2) That she should promise to take no more. (3) That she should unsay what she had said. 'For instance, you have said over and over that I lived in adultery these twenty years. Do you believe this or not? If you do, how can you think of living with such a monster. If you do not, give it me under your hand.'[32]

In the following year he wrote his last and saddest letter to his wife, saying that it was doubtful, considering their ages, if they would ever meet again in this life. He added in final desperation, 'If you were to live a thousand years, you could not undo the mischief that you have done. And till you have done all you can towards it, I bid you farewell.'[33]

In his Journal on 12 October 1781 there is a short note concerning Wesley's being informed of the death of his wife, a few days after the event, and of his being notified of the funeral after it had taken place. As a final gesture, Mary Wesley left John the wedding ring he had given her 30 years before.

Chapter 14

Social Concern

Wesley's social concern needs to be seen against a background of harsh working conditions, unemployment and poverty, on the one hand, and on the other hand a growth in philanthropy and social conscience. Throughout the eighteenth century life for poor people was difficult and dangerous. One Portuguese visitor, Manuel Gonzales, wrote of England, 'few nations are more burdened with them [the poor], there not being many countries where the poor are in a worse condition'.[1] Those who were unemployed or in prison, widows, orphans, and children born out of wedlock, were often condemned to a miserable life of destitution, hunger and ill-treatment. Even poor people who were employed were often forced to work long hours for little reward, made even smaller by unfair deductions from their pay. In the hosiery industry, for example, knitters had to rent their stocking frames, as well as having deductions from their meagre wages for needles and candles, coal and oil. They also had to bear the cost for collecting and delivering their work. Similarly, coal heavers unloading ships on the riverside in London had to hire their own shovels, while Cornish miners were forced to buy their candles from the mine owners. It was an age notorious for its drunkenness, thieving and prostitution. The situation is reflected in Charles Wesley's 'Conversion Hymn':

> Outcasts of men, to you I call
> Harlots, and Publicans, and Thieves! . . .
> He spreads his arms t'embrace you all
> Sinners alone his grace receives;

However, this was not the complete picture of life in the eighteenth century. The upward mobility of the population resulted in many people of good will coming together to found institutions and to promote societies that would affect and improve the lives of their fellow men and women. A notable example of this was the building of hospitals in London. At the beginning of the eighteenth century there were only two general hospitals in the capital, St Bartholomew's and St

Thomas's, and both were in financial difficulties due to a loss of income result-
ing from the destruction of properties in the Fire of London. However, subscriptions were soon raised for Guy's Hospital (1725), St George's (1733), and
the London Hospital (1740). Other specialist hospitals and homes were also
erected, such as the Lock Hospital (1746), for women with venereal disease, and
the Magdalen House (1758) for repentant prostitutes.[2]

This rising tide of philanthropy was not limited to England, but also found
expression in America and Europe, and took on many forms, such as the founding of the School for the Blind in Paris in 1784.

Wesley's social concern was part of this wider movement, although in his case
it was firmly grounded in his religious principles and evangelical aims. What is
impressive was the breadth of his activities, which embraced the relief of the poor,
support for prisoners, education and medical help for those who could not afford
it, and opposition to slavery. He supported these good causes by the generous use
of his time and his personal wealth, made possible through his careful stewardship of his resources and by adopting a frugal lifestyle. He had adhered to the
principle of living a simple life since his Oxford days, when, as a young man, he
had been challenged by his inability to help a poor girl because he had spent too
much on furnishing his rooms.[3]

Wesley's concern for poor people

Wesley set out the principles of his philanthropy in his sermon on 'The Use of
Money'. He urged his hearers to be progressive and entrepreneurial, and use their
God-given talents to acquire money. 'Gain all you can,' he told his hearers, 'it is
our bounden duty to do this.'[4] There were, however, cautions applied to this
process: the Christian must be honest and not endanger health or mind, or hurt
his neighbours.[5]

Second, he directed his hearers to 'Save all you can.' From his own experience
he implored his people to live simply and not to waste valuable resources, especially in order to gain admiration or the praise of others. His third rule was to
'Give all you can': 'You may as well throw your money into the sea, as bury it in
the earth. And you may as well bury it in the earth as in your chest, or in the
bank of England. Not to use, is effectually to throw it away.'[6] This was not only
what Wesley practised throughout his long life, but it was also what he preached.
'The Use of Money' was one of Wesley's favourite sermons; in his sermon regis-
ter, it appears 23 times. It was initially preached in 1744, although he did not
publish it until 26 years later. Wesley's need to repeat this sermon sprang from
his belief that a proper use of money was the real test of a person's Christian life.
He also felt that it was his duty to arouse the conscience of those who misused
money. This sermon illustrated the two elements of his Christian stewardship: its
use of money and time, which were gifts from God, and its responsibility to other
members of the community.

Wesley generously gave away the fortune he unexpectedly earned through his publications. At the age of 77 he wrote, 'I cannot help leaving my books behind me whenever God calls me hence; but in every other respect my own hands will be my executors.'[7] His favourite slogan of 'doing good' summed up his own attitude towards employing his resources. In order to satisfy himself that he was using his money effectively, and to be able to counter any wrongful allegations of the misuse of funds, he kept a careful account of all his expenditure and receipts over the years until just a few months before he died, by which time he was confident that he had lived up to his injunction of saving and giving all he could, 'that is, all I have'.[8]

From his early days as a Fellow of Lincoln College, Wesley had had a deep concern for the poor. His extensive travelling throughout the United Kingdom, and his meeting of people from all spheres of life, had given him a wider knowledge and understanding of their problems than many of his contemporaries. He strongly condemned the idea that people were only poor because they were lazy and refused to work. On 21 January 1740, four miles from Bristol at Lawford's Gate, he helped at least 150 people who were on the verge of starvation owing to the severe frosts that had prevented the breadwinners in each family from working. But it was not simply bad weather that could result in hunger; he found that many people, although working hard, could not earn sufficient money to support themselves and their families.

In London he came across people living and working in appalling conditions, with cold and hunger adding to their weakness and pain. But he discovered that many of them were employed, even those who were very ill or handicapped. Again, he railed against the common misapprehension, 'They are poor only because they are idle.'[9] In London in March 1753 he described the suffering:

> I visited more of the poor and sick. The industry of many of them surprised me. Several who were ill able to walk were nevertheless at work, some without any fire (bitterly cold as it was), and some, I doubt, without any food.[10]

It was scenes such as this that made him want to do something to help the poor. His extensive activities included making three collections to feed a large number of people in the Bristol area during the winter of 1740,[11] and the following winter he established a collection of clothes and went to considerable efforts to distribute them to poor and needy people. He also tackled the problem of seasonal working, which resulted in unemployment in the winter months. He provided employment for 12 of the poorest people by the spinning of cotton; he discovered that the cost of doing this was very little, as the workers could spin sufficient cotton to cover their own employment costs. What was needed, in fact, was organization rather than money.

None of these initiatives was sufficient to make a significant improvement among the poor, even within his own Societies. Thus, in 1741, Wesley called together members of the Methodist Society in London and highlighted the problems of those who lacked food, clothing and employment, or who were sick. He told them that he had done what he could, but realized it was insufficient to meet the need. He therefore made two proposals: that every member should donate one penny a week to help the poor and the sick; and that all spare clothing should be collected up to be given to the poor.[12] It was a scheme that quickly caught people's imaginations, as Wesley noted on his visit to Tetney in Lincolnshire:

> At noon I examined the little society at Tetney . . . In the class-paper (which gives an account of the contributions for the poor) I observed one gave eight pence, often ten pence, a week; another thirteen, fifteen, or eighteen pence; another, sometimes one, sometimes two shillings. I asked Micah Elmoor, the leader . . . 'How is this? Are you the richest society in all England?' He answered, 'I suppose not; but all of us who are single persons have agreed together to give both ourselves and *all we have* to God. And we do it gladly; whereby we are able, from time to time, to entertain all the strangers that come to Tetney, who often have no food to eat, nor any friend to give them a lodging.[13]

This kind of generosity was repeated again and again throughout the country, with the London Society, over a period of 20 years, collecting and giving to the poor some £14,000.[14]

Wesley was determined to build upon his experiment in providing employment, and thus undertook to employ any women who were out of work in the knitting trade. All recruits were given a basic wage, on top of which more money was provided by way of a means test. He then appointed 12 supervisors who could oversee this work and provide whatever was needed. These supervisors would also have the responsibility of visiting the sick in their areas every day.[15] In this way, Wesley created a self-help programme, which assisted those in real need while at the same time preserving their dignity and self-respect.

Wesley's charitable concerns did not develop as a carefully thought-out systematic plan to combat the evils of his day. They almost invariably arose when he was confronted by a particular need. His efforts were not directed at political change, but always towards the relief of individuals or groups of people. Throughout his life, even as an old man, he would go from door to door collecting money to feed and clothe the poor. In the week beginning 5 December 1785, at the age of 82, he spent every hour he could spare 'in the unpleasing but necessary work of going through the town and begging for poor men . . . if I do it not, nobody else will'.[16]

In a letter to Vincent Perronet, Wesley described how some of the more imaginative schemes for the relief of the poor were developed. One such project was his loan scheme. He noted that many people, especially those in business, needed to borrow money from time to time for short periods. Pawnbrokers and money lenders were expensive ways of raising the required finances, but there were few alternatives for poor people. He therefore decided to set up a loan fund whereby people could borrow up to twenty shillings to be repaid within a three-month period. Within a short time he had collected £50 for this purpose, and he noted with some satisfaction that in the first year 250 people had been helped by this fund.[17] Twenty years later the scheme was still flourishing and the capital sum was in excess of £120, with the borrowing limit raised to £5.

Wesley was not only collecting money and giving of his own resources to Methodist initiatives, but he was also moved to help humanitarian schemes outside his organization. The Strangers Friend Society was one such example, which was established by John Gardner, a retired soldier, to give money to those who could not get aid from parishes and had no friends to help them. Individuals were asked to subscribe one penny per week. Gardner, who found that his class leader opposed the scheme (no doubt because he felt it to be in conflict with the collections already being made by Methodists), wrote to Wesley to seek his approval. Wesley immediately supported the project and offered to subscribe three pence per week, and sent one guinea in advance, which more than doubled the fund. In the last year of his life, Wesley attended a meeting of the Society and noted with some pleasure that the Society continued to bring relief to the poor, the sick and the friendless strangers.[18] Gardner, probably under the influence of Wesley, went on to train as a doctor in order to be of further service to the poor.

Housing for widows and the sick was also another problem that Wesley decided to tackle. He took over two houses adjacent to the Foundry and provided a home for sixteen people, including nine poor widows, one blind woman and two children. When he and his preachers were in London they endeavoured to join the little company for meals. Wesley felt some pride that this initiative was, in a small way, modelled on the Early Church.[19]

For all his efforts, Wesley was not immune from criticism. In 1767 he received a letter blaming the Methodist Societies for having too much wealth and not sufficiently helping the poor. The letter criticized Wesley for failing to impress upon his followers their Christian obligation to care for those in need. Wesley replied, 'I do tell them so; and I tell them it will be more tolerable in the day of judgement for Sodom and Gomorrah than for them.'[20] A much more discerning appraisal was that of Joseph Priestley, the theologian and scientist of the Warrington Academy, who, although having a very different theology from Wesley, wrote, 'By you chiefly is the gospel preached to the *poor* in this country, and to you is the civilization, the industry and sobriety of great numbers of the laborious part of the community owing; though you are a body unknown to government, and look not for your reward from men.'[21]

Prison visiting

Prisons were also a major part of Wesley's social concern. He continued into old age the habit he had established at Oxford of visiting prisoners, especially those who were condemned to death. In the eight volumes of his Journal he recorded his constant visits to Newgate Prisons in London and Bristol, as well as the Marshalsea Prison and New Prison in London, and the Castle and Bocardo Prisons in Oxford. In visiting the Marshalsea Prison in 1753, he referred to it as 'a nursery of all manner of wickedness', and added, 'Oh shame to man that there should be such a place, such a picture of hell upon earth.'[22] His key interest lay with individual prisoners rather than in prison reform. His prison visiting was in part a response to the biblical injunction of Matthew 25, 'I was in prison and ye visited me', and partly due to his deep sympathy for individual prisoners, no doubt arising from his father's experience in Lincoln Prison.

The saving of souls was the primary motivation for Wesley's prison activities, but he was also concerned for the general well-being of prisoners, as can be seen from his encouragement of a Methodist, Abel Dagge, who was the jailer at Newgate Prison in Bristol. Dagge was originally drawn to Methodism through the preaching of George Whitefield in 1737. However, it was John Wesley who kept in touch with him, encouraged him, and visited the prison over the years. He was deeply affected by the improvements he saw Dagge making to Newgate. In 1760 he wrote a glowing account of Dagge's work,[23] which he saw as an outstanding example of the difference that one committed Christian could make even in the most desperate situation. Wesley noted that the whole prison had become 'as clean and sweet as a gentleman's house'. The prisoners took pride in the place and thoroughly cleaned the cells and the rooms of the prison twice a week. There was no fighting or brawling, as Dagge, who must have been a forceful character, settled every dispute on the spot, having listened to each side. Dagge eradicated cheating, drunkenness and prostitution, and other evils that tended to permeate the eighteenth-century prison scene. Within the prison he established cottage-type industries of shoe-making, tailoring and even coach building. He made every effort to provide all the tools and materials that were necessary to keep people employed and give them a sense of self-respect. On Sundays Dagge organized services of worship, which were compulsory for all inmates. Under his supervision, Newgate Prison in Bristol became a model of what prisons could be like. Wesley wrote of it: 'By the blessing of God on these regulations, the whole prison has a new face. Nothing offends either the eye or the ear, and the whole has the appearance of a quiet, serious family.'[24]

Dagge's single-handed reform of a prison from the inside pre-dated the efforts of John Howard to reform prison by legislation from the outside. Wesley was naturally an admirer of Howard's work. On Thursday 28 July 1787 the two men met in Dublin, and Wesley wrote of the meeting:

> I had the pleasure of a conversation with Mr Howard, I think one of the greatest men in Europe. Nothing but the mighty power of God can enable

him to go through his difficult and dangerous employments. But what can hurt us if God is on our side?[25]

Wesley was more aware than most clergy of the general conditions of prisons and the degradation of those incarcerated within them. He was often sent for by those who were condemned to death, and he invariably responded to such requests. Although he did not launch a national campaign for prison reform, he did succeed in raising the awareness of his followers and the wider public to a major social problem.

Education

John Wesley was also a passionate believer in the importance of education. He argued that education was for all, regardless of a person's age, wealth or place in society. His home background, his schooldays at Charterhouse, his education at Oxford, and his time as a Fellow of Lincoln College had all contributed to his interest in the subject. In addition to these influences, he made careful studies of the education theories and practices of others; he visited schools and universities, and set down his own ideas on education. He founded several schools and established programmes of adult learning.

The bands, classes and societies of Methodism served not only to develop spiritual growth and enforce discipline among the members, but they also became important educational channels. Once people joined the Methodist Societies, they were encouraged to learn to read, in order to read the Bible. Even those who could not read the Bible heard it being read, and the hymns they sang reinforced the biblical message. In this way, biblical imagery became part of their language for everyday life. Like the soldiers in the American Civil War, who wrote home from the front in beautiful biblical English, the conversation of Wesley's followers was steeped in biblical imagery. When Wesley met with the Methodist miners of Kingswood he wrote, 'The colliers spoke without any reserve. I was greatly surprised; not only the matter of what they spoke was rational and scriptural, but the language, yea, and the manner, were exactly proper.'[26]

The education of his preachers was another major concern for Wesley. To this end he organized reading parties and study groups similar to those held by Bishop King to help educate the clergy of the Lincoln diocese at the end of the following century. At one of these gatherings, at Kingswood School, he assembled as many preachers as he could and divided them into two groups: to the first group he read Bishop Pearson's *The Creeds*, and to the second group he read Aldrich's *Logic*. To the combined gathering he read *Rules of Action and Utterance*.[27] This Lenten gathering of 17 preachers was both devotional and educational, and was soon to be followed by similar meetings elsewhere. In London he gathered his preachers together and, surprisingly, read to them the abridged edition of the works of Francis Hutcheson (1694–1746), the late Professor of

Moral Philosophy at Glasgow. While Wesley admired the genius of the work, he also confessed to becoming increasingly unhappy with Hutcheson's approach to philosophy, which he felt was unsupported by Scripture.[28] Wesley would have found it difficult to accept Hutcheson's thesis that the standard of moral goodness was the promotion of the happiness of others. Considering his desire to control the education of his followers, it is interesting that Wesley was willing to read to his preachers books of which he did not approve.

The following month he again gathered his preachers together in London and read to them the *Procedure, Extent, and limits of Human Understanding* (1725) by Peter Browne, the late Bishop of Cork and Ross (d. 1735). This time he considered his chosen book to be 'excellent'.[29] Browne was opposed to John Toland's *Christianity not Mysterious* of 1696, which was widely disliked because of its deism. Browne would have been more orthodox than Hutcheson, a defender of the faith that Wesley passionately believed in.

Wesley also believed strongly in the importance of the printed word. He wrote, abridged and published a huge amount of literature for his preachers and his people to read. Some of it was sold, and some of it was given away. All of it was directed towards educational ends, increasing knowledge, and building up people in the Christian faith. One of his great aims was to produce inexpensive literature that would not be beyond the means of ordinary people. The range of his publications was enormous. They included English, French, Latin, Hebrew and Greek grammars, all of which sold for one penny, and *A Complete English Dictionary* and a *Concise History of England* in four volumes.

Every year, with few exceptions, he brought out several works. In 1745, for example, he produced an abridgement of Jonathan Edwards's *Thoughts on the Revival in New England* and *Extracts from Baxter's Aphorisms on Justification*. In the same year his and Charles's remarkable *Hymns on the Lord's Supper* came out. It was remarkable because it contained some of Charles Wesley's finest eucharistic hymns, and also because it contained (as a Preface) the abridged version of Dr Daniel Brevint's *The Christian Sacrament and Sacrifice*. In addition to these works, several tracts were published: *An Earnest Persuasion to keep the Sabbath day holy; A Word in Season or Address to an Englishman* (which was a call for loyalty to King George, in the year when many feared that England was to be overrun by the Pretender); *A Word to a Drunkard;* and *Advice to the People called Methodists*. It was also in this year that he produced the first section of his *Farther Appeal to Men of Religion and Reason*.

One of Wesley's most ambitious educational projects was his 'Christian Library', which he produced in the middle years of the century. His aim was to publish selections of the best works in the field of practical divinity. He chose works from a wide range of authors, such as Thomas Ken, Jeremy Taylor and John Tillotson, as well as some representatives of the Early Church such as Clement of Rome, Polycarp of Smyrna, and the Epistles of Ignatius of Antioch. Wesley set himself the task of abridging these works and making them available to a wide reading public. He wanted to encourage Methodists to read, believing that reading would give them a deeper knowledge of their faith. The production of his 'Christian Library' was a large task in which Wesley was generally faithful to the original authors in his abridgements. There were one or two notable exceptions. All references, for example, to Calvinists were omitted, and *Paradise Lost* was reduced by some 2,000 lines, which he thought would be too difficult for his readers to understand. Earlier he had also tampered with John Bunyan's work in an abridgement of *Pilgrim's Progress*, which actually included new material written by Wesley.[30]

Wesley did a great service to Christian education through his numerous publications. However, there is more than a hint that in producing all the writing himself he was exercising another form of control over the Methodist movement. He seldom seemed to have encouraged his preachers to write anything other than their Journals, and indeed forbade them to publish anything without his consent. When Cornelius Bayley requested Wesley's help to publish a book, Wesley pointed out that he and his brother Charles supplied most of the literary needs of Methodism.[31] However, Wesley did in fact help him to publish his *Hebrew Grammar*.

Wesley's schools

Wesley's social concern was also expressed in the care and education of children. He constantly instructed his preachers to pay special attention to children, and he had a strong desire to keep children from being corrupted. At Kingswood, three miles from Bristol, he founded four schools: two were single-sex charity schools and two were single-sex fee-paying schools. In addition to the Kingswood complex, he founded two charity schools, one in the Foundry in London, and the other in Bristol. He encouraged and supported others who established schools, and there were Methodist links to schools founded in Edinburgh, Dublin, Highgate, Weardale and Ironbridge.[32] Wesley's efforts to provide and encourage schools was part of the eighteenth-century drive for education, which was evident in the work of the SPCK, the establishment of Dissenting Academies, and the founding of the Royal Society of Arts (1758).

When Wesley built his first school at Kingswood he planned a simple structure with one large schoolroom and four small rooms, two of which were for the teachers. He also included in his design provision for adult education. It was his hope that people of all ages would attend classes at this school; but he did not think it was wise for older people to mix with younger children and, therefore, he planned that their education would take place in the early morning and in the evening after work.

The boys' boarding school at Kingswood is the only one of Wesley's schools to survive. This is not surprising since, in line with similar schools of the eighteenth century, they depended on individuals, so that when the proprietor or teacher either married, moved away or died, the school closed. Kingswood was Wesley's creation and, as Donald Tranter has aptly pointed out, he was proprietor, patron, governor, headmaster, director of studies, publicity and development officer, bursar and chaplain.[33] On 24 June 1748, when he opened the boys' boarding school at Kingswood, he preached on the text from Proverbs 22.6: 'Train up a child in the way he should go, and even when he is old he will not depart from it.' No child was permitted to join the school after the age of 12, as Wesley felt that by this age the youngster was too old to be influenced and would already be set in his ways.

The major aim of the school was the sharing of a common life of study, learning and worship under God. Every moment was God-given and, therefore, there were no holidays. Creative activities had to occupy each minute. The school day started at 4 a.m. with an hour of private reading or singing. From 5 a.m. to 6 a.m. the children went for walks, or took music lessons, or worked in the school garden. Breakfast, which largely consisted of porridge made with milk, was at 6 a.m., and school lessons under the instruction of teachers began at 7 a.m. The morning consisted of lessons in languages, writing and arithmetic until 11 a.m., with the last hour before lunch devoted to manual work or some kind of physical fitness. There was a simple lunch at 12 noon. The afternoon periods were taken up by the study of languages and other subjects, such as geography and physics. There was private prayer at 5 p.m., followed by more physical exercise at 6 p.m. A supper of bread and butter, cheese and milk was taken at 6.30 p.m. before evening worship at 7 p.m. All the children would go to bed at 8 p.m.

Although in his *Plain Account of Kingswood School*, Wesley maintained that he set higher standards than those generally found in the ancient universities,[34] he soon ran into trouble and found, as Newman was to discover in the next century, that running an educational institution was not easy:

> From the very beginning I met with all sorts of discouragements. Cavillers and prophets of evil were on every side. An hundred objections were made both to the whole design and every particular branch of it; especially by those from whom I had expected better things. Notwithstanding which, through God's help, I went on.[35]

In the early years it was hard to get pupils and difficult to appoint good staff. From 1748 until 1783, when Thomas McGeary took over, no headmaster could please Wesley for long, and he engaged a succession of poor housekeepers, including the infamous Sarah Ryan, who was reputed to have three husbands who were all still living.[36] The first two teachers he appointed were Robert Ramsey and Gwillam Snowde, who came to see him asking for work. They systematically embezzled the building fund, and were part-time highwaymen when off duty. They were eventually caught and tried, with Ramsey sentenced to death and Snowde deported. Both men independently sent messages to Wesley, requesting him to call and see them while in prison.

Wesley had a room in the school where he stayed when he visited Kingswood, and whenever he was there he did his best to encourage the pupils and members of staff. He was above all a man of great determination. Once he had put his mind to a task he pursued it with great vigour. This was true of great enterprises such as the school, but it was also true of smaller undertakings such as providing textbooks for the children. While staying at the school in 1756, between 27 September and 15 October, he wrote *A Short History of England* and *A Roman History*, and revised Kennet's *Antiquities of Rome*, Archbishop Potter's *Grecian Antiquities*, and Lewis's *Hebrew Antiquities*. He abridged Dr Cave's *Primitive Christianity*, and adapted Holmes's *Latin Grammar*.[37]

Wesley's concern for children was never mere lip-service. He gave generously of his money, his emotion, his energy and his love in all that he did for them. It must have cheered him greatly when, as an old man, children would run out into the streets in great numbers to see him passing by. One of the encouraging letters Wesley received came from Frances Owen, who wrote, 'The young folk heard that I am addressing you, Dear Sir, and with one voice beg to present their duty. They are counting the time when some of them hope to see you in Bristol.'[38]

Wesley's contribution to medicine

From his Oxford days and throughout the rest of his life, Wesley spent a great deal of time visiting the sick. From this experience he drew two conclusions: that poor people could not afford the medical treatment they needed, and that the doctors of his day often did little to cure their patients. In 1747 he wrote, 'I have had numberless proofs that regular physicians do exceeding little good.'[39] Having studied medicine himself for some 26 years in his 'leisure hours', first, because he felt that it would be helpful in America, and second, because of his great interest in the subject, he decided that he might be able to help those who were ill but had no access to a doctor. With this aim in mind, Wesley engaged the services of a dispensing chemist and an experienced surgeon, and solemnly resolved that he would not stray beyond his own knowledge.[40] Thus, on 5 December 1746 Wesley opened the Foundry doors in London to patients and began offering medical treatment to the poor each Friday. About 30 people came on the first day, and within three weeks he had seen some 300 people.[41] Within six months, the number had grown to about 600. The treatment was free and available to all, whether members of the Society or not, and the total cost borne by Wesley and the Society was estimated to be in excess of £40 over the six-month period.

One of the first to arrive was William Kirkman, a London weaver who had suffered from a bad cough and could get no rest at night. Wesley enquired:

'How long have you had it?' He replied 'About threescore years; it began when I was eleven years old.' I was nothing glad that this man should come first, fearing our not curing him might discourage others. However I looked up to God and said, 'Take this three or four times a day. If it does you no good, it will do you no harm'. He took it two or three days. His cough was cured, and he has not returned to this day.[42]

Wesley estimated that nine out of ten people who had taken the medicines he had prescribed were greatly improved within six weeks, and many were cured of diseases under which they had suffered for up to forty years.[43] Wesley soon opened two more dispensaries in Bristol and Newcastle.

In his important correspondence with 'John Smith', a pseudonym used by an educated person, Wesley felt obliged to defend his involvement in medicine. This he did with some style. Having first noted the success that he had already experienced, he then turned on Smith, asking if he should have sent these people away even though he knew how to cure them. He further noted that Smith was using as a convenience address the mansion of Dr Richard Mead in Great Ormond Street. Mead had been the physician to King George I and King George II, as well as Sir Isaac Newton and Sir Robert Walpole. Wesley asked Smith if he should have told these poor people to send for Dr Mead, for in all probability before Mead had arrived in his carriage the patient would have been in his coffin. In any case, who would have paid Mead's bill?[44]

Wesley was concerned that the medical knowledge he had acquired should be disseminated as widely as possible, so in 1747 he published his *Primitive Physic: or, An Easy and Natural Method of Curing Most Diseases*. It was to do for medicine in the eighteenth century what Mrs Beeton did for cookery and household management in the nineteenth century. *Primitive Physic* went into a total of 32 editions. The book was divided into two sections. The first dealt with preventative medicine and listed rules for good health. This section was largely based on Dr George Cheyne's book on *Health and Long Life*, which he had read earlier in his life, and contained the six themes of Cleanliness, Diet, Exercise, Sleep, Regular Habits and the Avoidance of Violent Stress. The second section of the book contained some 900 cures for 280 medical problems.[45]

Most of these 'cures' were well tried and tested and supported by medical knowledge and sound common sense. Other remedies were very dangerous, such as his advice to take three pounds of quicksilver for a twisted gut. In other cases he was quick to recognize and diagnose a problem such as scurvy, which was a common scourge in the eighteenth century, particularly among sailors. Wesley kept abreast of medical research and would have been aware of James Lind's *Treatise of the Scurvy* (1753); by 1780 Wesley was advocating the use of two Seville oranges and the taking every morning and evening of a spoonful or two of lemon juice and sugar as a cure.[46] It was almost the end of the century before the Royal Navy advocated taking lemons to sea, and several years later before the cause of scurvy was discovered to be a lack of vitamin C.

Wesley was also a great enthusiast for the use of electrotherapy for nervous problems. Together with Dr Lovett of Worcester, he can be considered a pioneer of this form of treatment, which he also used for treating epilepsy, angina and cramp. He started using electrotherapy in November 1756, having obtained the apparatus for this purpose. Some of his patients found immediate cure, while others improved gradually. He made the treatment available so that 'any that desire it might try the virtue of this surprising medicine'. Within two years the patients were so numerous that he had to establish three more centres for treatment in London.[47]

Wesley was not without his critics concerning this sort of treatment – one of whom was the great Dr Joseph Priestley who, in *The History and Present State of Electricity with Original Experiments* (1767), criticized Wesley and Lovett for not having the medical knowledge to diagnose the disorder accurately or assess the seeming cure in using electrotherapy. Priestley did, however, hand out a guarded compliment to the two men when he remarked that if so much good and so little harm had been done by unskilled hands, the potential for electrotherapy in more skilful hands was very great indeed.[48]

Another contemporary critic of Wesley's general approach set out in *Primitive Physic* was a London physician, Dr William Hawes, who in *Lloyd's Evening Post* on 22 July 1776 referred to Wesley's work as that of a 'dangerous quack'. However, his criticism merely served to draw attention to *Primitive Physic*, which resulted in greatly increased sales. Wesley wrote to him, 'Dear Sir, My bookseller informs me that since you published your remarks on the *Primitive Physick* [sic] there has been a greater demand for it than ever. If, therefore, you would please to publish a few farther remarks, you would confer a farther favour upon Your humble servant.'[49]

Wesley also was able to recognize psychosomatic illness, as shown when he attended a woman who had no relief from the drugs prescribed for her stomach pains. On making careful enquiries, he discovered that she was grieving for the loss of her son. Dr Wesley Hill, commenting on this story, says, 'Few eighteenth-century doctors would have thought of relating stomach pain to emotional distress.'[50]

Much of Wesley's contribution to medicine was, by today's standards, common sense. He advocated plenty of exercise, eating sparingly, avoiding tea or spirits, cleanliness of the home and person, and getting sufficient sleep. His success was also due to his careful observation, his ability to listen, and a genuine desire to 'do good' to others. Dr Robert Parry, one-time Medical Officer of Health for the City of Bristol, when referring to the nineteenth-century social reformer Edwin Chadwick, wrote, 'He did not start that fight, of course. One hundred years before him John Wesley fought his great fight for hygiene; he was the greatest health educator of the eighteenth century in Britain.'[51]

Wesley and the slave trade

A deep concern that occupied Wesley up to the last days of his life was that of the abolition of the slave trade. He was not the first nor the major opponent of slavery, but he was well informed of the situation, and deeply moved by the plight of slaves; and he added his considerable voice and energy towards achieving the desired outcome. The Quakers were the early opponents of slavery, and in the seventeenth century they were raising their voices against what they considered to be an unjust and wicked system. As early as 1727 they publicly called for its abolition.

Although Wesley had taken a keen interest in the well-being and education of people of African origin while he was in America and on the journey home, he did not publicly enter the debate on the slave trade until the 1770s. While travelling from Dorking back to London in February 1772, he read a book on slavery (probably *A Historical Account of Guinea*) by Anthony Benezet, a Quaker. From the comments in Wesley's Journal it appears that up to this time he was unaware of the horrors endured by slaves, but from that point on he branded it as 'that execrable sum of all villainies, commonly called the Slave-trade'.[52] But, like everything else he did, once he had turned his mind to something he pursued it with great vigour. Within two years he had entered the arena, first, with a letter written to the editor of the *Monthly Review* protesting against the treatment of slaves, and second, by a very carefully argued treatise, *Thoughts on Slavery* (1774).[53]

Wesley's *Thoughts on Slavery* was very moving and a well-argued piece of writing. He referred to slavery as 'an obligation of perpetual service which only the consent of the master can dissolve, and moreover which allows the master to alienate the slave, in the same manner as his cows or horses'. He also noted that it descended from parent to child. He then described the countries from which the slaves came, and contrasted their former lives with their cruel capture, branding, and inhumane transportation. In the capturing of slaves he estimated that 30,000 people were 'murdered' each year: 'It is common for several hundred of them to be put on board one vessel, where they are stowed together in as little room as it is possible for them to be crowded. It is easy to suppose what condition they must soon be in, between heat, thirst, and stench of various kinds. So that it is no wonder that so many should die in the passage; but rather, that any survive it.'[54] He went on to argue that neither captivity nor contract could by the plain law of nature or by reason reduce a person to slavery. Nor, according to Wesley, could a person be born into slavery.

He strongly hit out against the economic argument that only black slaves could work in hot climates and argued that white people could adapt to hot climates by degrees. He then asked the interesting question of where the opposition against slavery should be directed. He came to the conclusion that this should not be at governments or the general public, but at those most closely involved:

the captains, the traders and the owners of slaves, to whom he made an appeal, 'Let none serve you but by his own act and deed, by his own voluntary choice.' His final paragraph was a prayer to God to intervene, 'Thou Saviour of all, make them free, that they may be free indeed.'[55] Wesley ensured that this paper was published and widely distributed.

In August 1787 Wesley wrote to the newly formed Committee for the Abolition of the Slave Trade to inform the members of his great satisfaction that this committee had come into being. Wesley believed that its objective would not only abolish the slave trade, but would strike at the very heart of 'the shocking abomination of slavery' itself.[56] But he warned the members that they must expect difficulties and great opposition in this undertaking and that all sorts of evil things would be done to them. Later that year he wrote to Thomas Funnell offering to give whatever help he could to those who had joined together to oppose the slave trade. Again, he warned that there would be 'vehement opposition, both by slave merchants and slave-holders; and they are mighty men'.[57] He told Funnell that one practical thing that he would do was to have a large edition of his *Thoughts on Slavery* reprinted and distributed to all parts of England. In the spring of the following year, approaching the age of 85, Wesley, like an old warhorse sensing the smell of battle, set out for Bristol, and on 6 March, in a city that owed so much to the slave trade, he preached against slavery. At the end of his sermon he declared that the following day would be a day of prayer and fasting in remembrance of slaves.[58]

Wesley was concerned with the issue of slavery for the remaining years of his life. Not long before his death he subscribed to the publication entitled *The Interesting Narrative of the Life of Olaudah Equiano, or Gustavus Vassa*. It was the story of Vassa, who had been born in Africa in 1745. He was later captured and sold as a slave in Barbados and transported to Virginia. However, his master sent him to England in 1757, and two years later he was baptized in St Margaret's Church, Westminster. From then onwards he had several adventures in the Royal Navy and in the West Indies.

Wesley had just received the book and was reading it on his way to Leatherhead; it turned out to be the last book that he read. He was greatly moved by it, and on his return home felt inspired to write what was to become his last letter, to William Wilberforce, to encourage him in his crusade to abolish slavery within the British Empire. Wesley wrote:

> Unless God has raised you up for this very thing, you will be worn out by the opposition of men and devils. But 'if God be for you, who can be against you?' Are all of them together stronger than God? O 'be not weary in well doing!' Go on, in the name of God and in the power of his might, till even American slavery (the vilest that ever saw the sun) shall vanish away before it.
>
> Reading this morning a tract, wrote by a poor African, I was particularly

struck by that circumstance, – that a man who has a black skin, being wronged or outraged by a white man, can Have no redress; it being a law, in all our colonies, that the oath of a black against a white goes for nothing. What villany is this.

That He who has guided you from your youth up, may continue to strengthen you in this and all things, is the prayer of, Dear Sir,

Your affectionate servant[59]

Wesley, as we have seen, was a man of immense kindness and generosity. It was not any one individual act of social concern that endeared him to people, but, taken together, these acts show a man who was deeply concerned for his fellow men and women, who captured their imagination, and made them feel that there was goodness in the world and that they wanted to be part of it.

Chapter 15

Farewell

Over the last few years of his life Wesley developed the habit of recording his health on his birthday, which, owing to the change in the calendar, he celebrated on 28 June each year. These records make interesting reading. At the age of 77 he felt like a man of 28. Two years later, he wrote that he felt like a man of 25. The next year, however, he was comparing himself to a man of 50, while in the following year, 1784, at the age of 81, he considered his physical health to be equivalent to a person of 21! Wesley ascribed his excellent health to exercise, early rising and preaching. Almost to the very end of his life his enormous energy and unceasing activity continued unabated, and Midsummer's Day 1786 serves as a good example of a normal day's work for him. He had stayed the previous night in Gainsborough, and rose in the early hours of the morning to pray and write a sermon. By 5.30 a.m. he was setting off in a chaise for Newton-on-Trent. On arrival, at 8 a.m., he took tea and then preached on Psalm 10.12. From Newton he travelled on to Newark for lunch at 12 noon. After the meal he preached on Ecclesiastes 9.10. At 2.45 p.m. he set out for Tuxford, where he spent half-an-hour with the people before travelling on to Retford to preach and say prayers at 6.15 p.m. This was followed by supper in the company of his hosts and evening prayer in the family home, which he conducted before retiring to bed at 9.30 p.m.[1] Four days later, on his eighty-third birthday, he recorded, 'I am never tired (such is the goodness of God!) either with writing, preaching, or travelling.'[2]

Wesley was almost 85 before he began to record in his Journal his failing health. He noted in the spring of that year that he walked slower, his memory was not so quick, and that he found it more difficult to read by candlelight.[3] Fifteen months later, on his eighty-sixth birthday, he noted with some sadness that his sight had 'decayed', his strength had declined, and his memory for persons, places and names was not as good as it used to be. His concern seemed to be that he did not want to lose his mental faculties and become a burden on others, or a stubborn and grumpy old man. He had no need to worry about either of these two things happening, though, because he continued to be the cheerful companion that he had always been, and retained his mental faculties to the end of his days.

In the last years of his life he displayed enormous determination to continue his demanding regime of travelling and preaching, even when his health was failing and he was becoming very frail. People who display such determination can often be very difficult to live with when younger, but in old age are generally seen as great figures, looked upon with admiration and affection. Wesley always enjoyed the company and conversation of others and was kept active in old age by the warm companionship he had found in the large family of Methodism that he had created. The older he got, the more popular he became; people lined the streets, crowded into windows to see him, and greeted him as he passed by. Wesley showed a real modesty and humility in his old age: he enjoyed the fellowship more than the admiration. Richard Watson, in his life of Wesley, noted that when Wesley passed through the towns and villages of Cornwall, the windows were crowded with people anxious to see him and to pronounce their blessing on him, and yet he made no mention of this in his Journal or letters.[4]

The last seven years of his life were dominated by three major events: the establishing of the 'Legal Hundred' for the continuation of Methodism; the ordaining of ministers for the American ministry; and the death of his brother Charles.

The establishment of the 'Legal Hundred'

As Wesley became older there was increasing concern among the preachers and members of Methodism about what would happen after his death. Wesley himself had taken the initiative to solve the problem as early as 1773, and had written to his great friend and supporter John Fletcher, the Vicar of Madeley, requesting him to be the next leader of the Methodist people. Unfortunately, Fletcher's health collapsed in 1777 and, when he arrived at the Methodist Conference of that year, many were shocked by his appearance as he showed all the signs of someone who was gravely ill. Several burst into tears as he spoke, and Wesley knelt beside him as the Conference prayed that he might be restored to health. From that moment onwards it became apparent that another solution would be needed for the continuation of Methodism. Fletcher's health was not up to the challenge and in the end (1785) it fell to Wesley to preach his funeral sermon.[5]

Thus, in February 1784, Wesley was faced with the issue of defining the Governing Body of Methodism, and for this purpose he drew up the Deed of Declaration, which named the 100 members of the Methodist Conference, which later became known as the 'Legal Hundred'. The Deed contained 16 rules that defined how the Conference was to operate. These included the instructions that it had to meet once a year for not less than five days and not more than three weeks. The act of the majority was to be the act of the whole, and the Conference could only appoint persons to use the chapels of Methodism who were either members of the Conference, or in connection with the Conference, or were preachers on trial, or were ordained members of the Church of England. There is a clear indication here that Wesley wanted Methodism to remain part of the Church of England.

The Deed of Declaration, although solving one problem, created another. There were at this time 191 preachers in Methodism, but only 100 were to be members of the Conference. Although Wesley drew up the list naming the first 100 members, it was not apparent that this selection had been done on the basis of seniority or any other rational system, with the result that several whose names did not appear felt bitterly disappointed. This action caused a minor crisis within Methodism as, prior to the Deed of Declaration, all 191 members had considered themselves to be full members of the Conference. Almost half the preachers, therefore, felt themselves to be suddenly disenfranchised. The crisis passed over with the resignation of five preachers who were opposed to the Deed: John Atlay, William Eels, the two John Hampsons, and Joseph Pilmoor. If Wesley had listened to the advice of his friend, Thomas Coke, he would have included the names of all the preachers and would have retained the services of good men such as John Hampson (Senior), who had served him faithfully.

Ordaining men for the American ministry

The other issue that Wesley faced at this time was that of ordaining ministers for the American ministry. During the War of Independence the number of American Methodists had grown rapidly, from 2,074 in 1774 to 15,000 or so ten years later. By the end of the War of Independence there were 46 circuits, 83 travelling preachers, and 100 local preachers. The collapse of British resistance after 1780 in the American War of Independence and the withdrawal of British troops from Charleston and Savannah resulted in the leaders of the Church of England being less interested in America. Wesley tried unsuccessfully to persuade Bishop Lowth of London to ordain men for America. The situation was brought to a head when Francis Asbury wrote to Wesley pointing out some of the problems faced by Methodists in America due to the shortage of ministers. Many members had not received the Lord's Supper for several years and thousands of children remained unbaptized.[6] On 20 March 1784, Asbury wrote again to ask Wesley to come to America, which he believed would greatly please a large number of people.[7]

Wesley decided to act. As early as 1746, on his way to Bristol, he had read Peter King's *An Enquiry into the Constitution, Discipline, and Unity, and Worship of the Primitive Church*, which had satisfied him that in the Early Church 'bishops and presbyters are (essentially) of one order'.[8] King was a 21-year-old Presbyterian when he wrote his treatise, but he later joined the Church of England and went on to become Lord Chancellor. It was surprising that Wesley was willing to give so much credence to *Primitive Church* when there were many well-argued replies to King, whose whole thesis went against the general consensus of opinion in the Church of England. Moreover, Wesley had run into difficulties and severe criticism over the issue of ordination when, some twenty years previously, in 1764, he had enlisted the services of a Greek Orthodox bishop, Erasmus of Arcadia, to ordain some of his lay preachers.

But the situation in America was critical, so Wesley decided to carry out his plan. At the end of the summer of 1784, in a room in Bristol, Wesley 'set apart', 'appointed' or 'ordained' (the certificate, the Journal, and the Diary all use different words) the Reverend Dr Thomas Coke as superintendent of 'the People in the Southern Provinces of North America who desire to continue under my care and still adhere to the Doctrines and Discipline of the Church of England'. The following day Wesley ordained Richard Whatcoat and Thomas Vasey to accompany Coke and promote the work in America.

In a letter to the Methodists in America, Wesley gave a detailed account of his actions:

> But the case is widely different between England and North America. Here there are bishops who have a legal jurisdiction; in America there are none, neither any parish minister; so that, for some hundreds of miles together, there is none either to baptise, or to administer the Lord's Supper. Here, therefore, my scruples are at an end, and I conceive myself at full liberty, as I violate no order and invade no man's right by appointing and sending labourers into the harvest . . .
>
> I have accordingly appointed Dr Coke and Mr Francis Asbury to be joint superintendents over our brethren in North America, as also Rich. Whatcoat and T. Vasey, to act as elders among them, by baptising and administering the Lord's Supper. And I have prepared a liturgy, little differing from that of the Church of England (I think the best constituted National Church in the world), which I advise all travelling preachers to use on the Lord's Day . . .[9]

As the three – Coke, Whatcoat and Vasey – sailed from England for America on 18 September 1784 a new chapter in church history had begun, both for the New World and the old. It was not long before Asbury and Coke were calling themselves bishops, and the Methodist Societies in America were taking on an independent life of their own. Wesley was shocked: 'How can you, how dare you, suffer yourself to be called Bishop. Men may call me a knave or a fool . . . and I am content; but they shall never by my consent call me Bishop!'[10] But his objections fell upon deaf ears.

At home Wesley's actions were to become the decisive step that would eventually lead to the separation of the Methodist Societies from the Church of England. Charles Wesley, who was greatly upset by his brother's conduct, made no secret of his displeasure both to his friends and to John. He succinctly put his thoughts in rhyme:

> Wesley on Coke his hands hath laid,
> But who laid hands on him?

The letters between the two brothers argued the case from both sides, but in the end their love and friendship for each other was to transcend even this difference. Charles finished his correspondence on 8 September 1785 with the touching comment, 'I thank you for your intention of remaining my friend. Herein my heart is as your heart . . . We have taken each other for better or worse, till death us do part – part? no; but unite eternally. Therefore in the love that never faileth, I am your affectionate friend and brother.'[11]

Charles Wesley's death

Charles must have known when he wrote this letter that they could not have much longer to enjoy one another's company and support. He would have been aware that his own health and strength were failing. John must have noticed it as well. Shortly before Christmas 1787 it became evident that Charles was not well and had largely confined himself to his home,[12] and in a letter of February 1788 John begged Charles not to make any financial economies that could be detrimental to his health and promised to meet any doctors' bills.[13] In subsequent letters he sent Charles a report on the work in Bath and pleaded with him not to die simply to save expense. He also assured Charles that there was more work for him to do.

In 1788, not long before he died, Charles wrote his last hymn, the final verse of which reads:

> O that the joyful hour was come
> Which calls Thy ready servant home,
> Unite me to the church above,
> Where angels chant the song of love
> And saints eternally proclaim
> The glories of the heavenly Lamb![14]

He then sent for the minister of St Marylebone Parish Church and told him that he had lived, and would die, a communicant of the Church of England and that he wished to be buried in the churchyard. On 29 March 1788 Charles Wesley died, surrounded by his family. John was staying at Madeley at the time and, although a letter was despatched from London informing him of the sad news, he did not receive it until the day of the funeral. By then it was too late for him to return to London in time for the service, so he immediately wrote a letter to Charles's widow, Sarah, offering all the help he could to her and her family.

The death of Charles not only marked the end of a unique pattern of leadership within the Christian Church, but it was also the end of a remarkable friendship and brotherly love, which stretched back over the decades of the century to Epworth and Oxford, across the Atlantic and in the New World. John, who in times of crisis and heartbreak always continued to work, nevertheless felt the loss of Charles deeply. Preaching in Bolton two weeks later he announced Charles's hymn, 'Come O, Thou Traveller unknown', but when he read the words 'My company before is gone, And I am left alone with Thee', he completely broke down, burst into tears, and sat down in the pulpit, burying his face in his hands.[15] He eventually managed to continue the service.

It was a moving and never-to-be-forgotten moment for those who were present in the congregation. It was also a clear indication of how much the two brothers had meant to each other, although John was disappointed that Charles had chosen to be buried in his parish churchyard rather than in the New Chapel they had built in City Road in 1776 as the centre of their London work. It was a mark of his deep love for Charles that John resolved to write his brother's biography. Although this work was never completed due to his limited time and old age, there are references in his Journal to making a start on this project[16] and to reading his brother's works.[17] John would have been made deeply conscious of the genius of Charles's hymn-writing, and of its importance to Methodism, when he had been compiling the 'Large Hymn Book' ten years previously. The 1780 *Collection of Hymns for the Use of the People called Methodists* contains 525 hymns, the vast majority of which were written by Charles.

The final steps

As old age and infirmity crept up on John, it made little difference to his pattern of life. Occasionally, he would lie in bed until 4.30 a.m. instead of 4 a.m., but in general it did not seem greatly to reduce his travelling, preaching or letter writing. It was also interesting that in old age he received more invitations to preach in parish churches than he could possibly accept. Nor did his healthy outlook on life or his optimism diminish. On 1 January 1789, he wrote, 'If this is to be the last year of my life, according to some of those prophecies, I hope it will be the best.'[18]

His intellect and enthusiasm did not diminish in these last years, and he continued to show a great interest in everything. He was delighted on a visit to Bolton to discover that George Eskrick had founded a Sunday school for 800 poor children. About eighty masters gave of their time free of charge and the children were taught to read and write. One hundred of them were taught to sing, and they sang like angels before Wesley addressed them. It was a great mark of Wesley's effect on the children that many of them refused to go home while he was still there and hovered about the building until the evening. Wesley called them together and asked them to sing again. Although some could not sing because of the tears in their eyes, these poor children of Bolton sang so beautifully that Wesley believed the choir of King's College Chapel could not equal them.[19] Within a few years, the Bolton Sunday school was educating in excess of 2,000 children.

The last pages of his Journal not only record his preaching to great crowds in newly opened chapels that could not contain the congregation, but also described the beautiful scenery he passed through, such as that between Hexham and Haltwhistle, 'one of the pleasantest countries I have lately seen'.[20] He included other things he came across on his journeys, such as in Chester where he stayed at the home of a Mr Sellers. His host had in his yard a large Newfoundland dog and an old raven. Wesley was amazed to discover that the bird and the dog had fallen deeply in love and could not bear to be parted from one another. The old bird could imitate the bark of the dog and was inconsolable whenever the dog went out. If he was away for a day or so, she would gather all the bones and scraps of food she could find and keep them ready for his return.[21] The Journal also gives an indication that towards the end of his life he became nostalgic about his own childhood. On 30 November 1789 he visited a Mr Smith at Cuddesdon, who had ten children between the ages of one and eighteen, reminding him of his own childhood and family life at Epworth.[22]

Although in the last year of his life his right hand badly shook, his letter writing continued unabated: he wrote several letters a day. Among the many letters he wrote in June 1790 was one to the Bishop of Lincoln, requesting him not to drive Methodists out of the Church of England. He wrote, 'Methodists in general, my Lord, are members of the Church of England. They hold her doctrines, attend her services, and partake of her sacraments.' He concluded the letter with a heartfelt appeal:

O my Lord, for God's sake, for Christ's sake, for pity's sake suffer the poor people to enjoy their religious as well as civil liberty. I am on the brink of eternity! Perhaps so is your Lordship too! How soon may you also be called to give an account of your stewardship to the Great Shepherd and Bishop of our souls! May He enable both you and me to do it with joy![23]

In the last two months of his life he wrote in excess of 30 letters, which are preserved, all of them written in clear, beautiful English. One of them was his last letter to America, addressed to Ezekiel Cooper of Philadelphia and written three weeks before John Wesley died. It expressed his desire for a united Methodist movement. He wrote, 'Lose no opportunity of declaring to all men that the Methodists are one people in all the world; and that it is their full determination so to continue.'[24]

Wesley made his usual travelling arrangements for the new year, 1791. He planned to start his journeys on the last day of February. On 17 February, however, after preaching at Lambeth, he was taken ill. Although he struggled to keep several of his appointments, by Sunday 19 February, after rising early, he was very weak and forced to return to his bed for several hours. However, he seemed much better on the Monday and so travelled to Twickenham, and on the following day he preached at City Road. On Wednesday 22 February he set out to Leatherhead at the invitation of a well-to-do family, and preached in their home on the text 'Seek ye the Lord, while He may be found, call ye upon Him while He is near'.

This was his last sermon. On his way home to City Road he stayed the night with his old friend, George Wolff, at Balham, where he wrote his last letter, addressed to William Wilberforce. On arriving back at his home in City Road, it was obvious that he was unwell. He had difficulty getting out of his carriage, and even more difficulty climbing the stairs. From then on he stayed in his room; he spoke little and slept a great deal. As the evening of his life drew in, his friends and family gathered round his bed, including Sarah, Charles's widow, and her daughter Sarah. On one occasion he asked for pen and paper, but could not write. On the afternoon before he died he amazed his friends and family by singing two verses of Isaac Watts's hymn, 'I'll praise my maker while I have breath'. Later that evening he uttered the words that became a motto for Methodism, 'The best of all is God is with us', and the next morning, at 10 a.m. on 2 March, he spoke the one word 'Farewell' and died peacefully.

He had requested a simple funeral, but tens of thousands of people filed past his open coffin in the City Road Chapel. Those charged with the responsibility of the funeral had tried to avoid great crowds by announcing only the evening before that the funeral would take place at 5 a.m. on the following morning. Nevertheless, his friends and followers flocked to the service. While conducting the ceremony, John Richardson changed the words of the burial rite from 'brother' to 'father', and read 'For as much as it hath pleased Almighty God to take unto Himself the soul of our dear *Father* here departed'. There was hardly a dry eye among the members of the congregation. Few who were present could remember a time when Wesley had not been on the national scene, preaching to large crowds, caring for people, and encouraging the Methodist movement.

With Wesley's death the old world seemed to be passing away. Europe was in the throes of revolution and soon to be in the grip of Napoleon. America was making its own newly independent way in the world. In Britain, the Industrial Revolution was to gain momentum with the growth of large factories and mills, industrial towns and cities, railways and roads. The green and pleasant country-side of Britain and Ireland in Wesley's day was soon to be lost in the industrial smoke and grime of a new age.

Assessing the impact of John Wesley

Any assessment of Wesley would have to acknowledge that there were great fail-ures throughout his life. Most notably, he failed in his marriage and in his mis-sionary endeavours in America. The Methodist movement could not do for the

English Church what the Jesuits were able to do for the Church of Rome. He failed to retain the American Methodists within his organization, and even before his death they were striking out on their own. Although he was good at winning converts, he failed to some extent to hold on to them, as his last visits to Epworth and Misterton suggest, where the Societies retained only 'the shadow of their former zeal and activity'.[25] He also failed to take the necessary steps to keep the Methodist Societies within the Church of England.

His frank correspondence with his brother Charles, in 1766, suggests that at times he was racked with doubts and had failed in his own life to experience the faith that he was preaching. He wrote, 'And yet this is the mystery, I do not love God. I never did . . . Therefore I never *believed* in the Christian sense of the word. Therefore I am only an honest heathen . . .'[26] It is difficult to tell from this letter whether he was referring to a temporary doubt or whether this was something he wrestled with over a lifetime. Such self-doubt and times of failure were deeply human experiences, which must have contributed to making him a great preacher and a lovable man, and not just a cleric and an administrator. Even in the face of failure he never gave up or lost heart. He was still, in the words of E. P. Thompson, 'a great-hearted war horse, who had never spared himself; he was an enthusiast who had stood up at the market-cross to be pelted'.[27]

On the other hand, his work must be recognized as having had a profound effect in many ways. He preached the love of God and brought faith and good works together in a manner in which few evangelical leaders have managed to do before or since. It is one of the glories of Wesley's Methodism that his spirituality always found expression in material things and in 'doing good'. He drew attention to the iniquities of his day, as when he came across an old woman 'who had been glad to make a meal out of an old bone which a dog had found'. And this, he said, 'is a land flowing with milk and honey'.[28] He not only described such things, but was determined to do something about them. His initiatives in health, education, prisons, and feeding and clothing the poor, were all part of his two-pronged approach of faith and works.

Wesley's distinctive response to the world he found in eighteenth-century Britain was to inspire men and women to lead lives that were dedicated to worship, social care and personal holiness to a degree that was unusual in the Church of England of his day. When he died, it was natural that those men and women wanted, and needed, to carry on the patterns of holy living and holy dying that they had learned from their 'Father in God'. The Church that followed, and grew (and divided) in the nineteenth century, was a direct consequence of Wesley's own vision, even though its independence from the Church of England was never his original intention. But the steps he took in 1784 made a separate Church inevitable.

He helped to change the climate of opinion in Great Britain and Ireland. Through his and his brother's hymns, which people sang in their homes as well as in church, through his preaching, and through belonging to his Societies with their various rules of behaviour, he helped men and women to capture a different and better vision of what life could be like. These changes came about not only through his teaching, but also by his example of genuine goodness.

Wesley changed the lives of individuals. He gave poor people a sense of value and worth and reminded them that they too were children of God. Through his efforts, keelmen and miners, prostitutes and prisoners, sailors and smugglers, all became devout people with a purpose in life, and valued in society. This is another way of seeing the influence of Methodism, contrary to the viewpoint put forward by E. P. Thompson.[29] Thompson's concentration on the unhealthy side of Methodism has obscured the fact that, for many people, Methodism was a source of life and purpose, a 'solution' both in physical and spiritual terms. It saved men and women from poverty, aimlessness and degradation, and gave them a glimpse of heaven. It taught them to hope in the hereafter, but it also made them stable parents, good citizens and caring people.

So what was the secret of Wesley's success? It is important to remember first of all that Wesley was an intellectual, and there is no doubt that at Oxford he built on the intellectual foundation laid by his mother. Whatever the other benefits of an Oxford education, at its best Oxford taught its scholars to read, write, think for themselves, and to defend an argument. Wesley was not simply a travelling evangelist: he was a highly educated theologian who had carefully thought out his own position on the great issues of life and death. He had studied the major theologians and saints of the past and was able to preach well-thought-out sermons to the University of Oxford, hold his own in discussions with Bishop Butler, the leading philosopher of the day, and with Dr Johnson, the outstanding man of letters of his time, who enjoyed his company.

Second, Wesley exhibited a profound social concern. He was deeply interested in people and their material well-being, especially the poor and children. Likewise, he gave unstintingly of his own money to those in need. Wherever goodness, kindness and generosity are shown, there will be those who recognize that the spirit of God is at work.

Third, one must never forget Wesley's sheer dedication, and his profound belief that he was carrying out the work of God. He is a clear example of how one dedicated person can have an influence on national life. He awakened people to the simple truth of Christianity: that it meant loving God with all their hearts and loving their neighbours with the same love that God had shown to them.

Finally, Wesley's success was due to the fact that he propounded an idea whose time had come. The evangelical revival broke out not only in England, but also in Germany and America. When Samuel and Susanna, John Wesley's parents, looked out of the windows of the rectory at Epworth on to a world that must have seemed very hostile to Christianity, they would have found it difficult to believe that their sons, John and Charles, would be in the forefront of a great religious revival that would call men and women back to holiness, and help to prepare the Christian Church to face the challenges and opportunities of the future.

Notes

Chapter 1   Susanna and Samuel

1 Lee, Umphrey, *The Lord's Horseman: John Wesley the Man* (London, 1956), p.1; Newton, John, *Susanna Wesley* (London, 1968), p. 68.

2 Beecham, H. A., 'Samuel Wesley Senior: New Biographical Evidence', in *Renaissance and Modern Studies* (Nottingham, 1963), vol. VII, p. 89.

3 It was as a mark of respect and affection for Dolling that Samuel dedicated his first publication to him.

4 Clarke, Adam, *Memoirs of the Wesley Family*, 2 vols (London, 1836), vol. I, p. 97.

5 Beecham, 'Samuel Wesley Senior', p. 103.

6 Beecham, 'Samuel Wesley Senior', p. 164.

7 Wallace, Charles, Jr, ed., *Susanna Wesley: The Complete Writings* (Oxford, New York, 1997), p. 153.

8 Wallace, *Susanna Wesley: The Complete Writings*, p. 71.

9 Adam Clarke describes Dunton as 'the famous eccentric bookseller' as well as publisher.

10 Wakeley, J. B., *Anecdotes of the Wesleys* (London, 1889), p. 21.

11 Beecham, 'Samuel Wesley Senior', p. 91.

12 Wakeley, *Anecdotes of the Wesleys*, p. 22.

13 Beecham, 'Samuel Wesley Senior', pp. 89–90. It is also interesting that there is no record of the baptism of two daughters born at South Ormsby: another Susanna, who married Mr Ellison, and Mary, who became the wife of Mr Whitelamb.

14 Newton, *Susanna Wesley*, p. 75.

Chapter 2   Epworth and the Rectory

1 McClure, Edmund, ed., *A Chapter in English Church History: being the Minutes of the Society for Promoting Christian Knowledge* (London, 1888), p. 345.

2 Richard Heitzenrater has done valuable research on this in his book *John Wesley and the People called Methodists* (Nashville, 1995).

3 Rack, Henry, *Reasonable Enthusiast: John Wesley and the Rise of Methodism* (London, 1989), p. 49.

4 Clarke, Adam, *Memoirs of the Wesley Family*, 2 vols (London, 1836), vol. I, pp. 190–3.

5 On arriving at Epworth it had cost Samuel a further £50 to get the Great Seal as this was a Crown appointment; moreover, he needed £50 to pay off his main creditors. At Epworth he had to furnish his house, costing a further £50, pay his taxes of £20 per year, support his aged mother at £10 per year, and rebuild his barns when they collapsed – an additional expense of £40.

6 Wallace, Charles, Jr, ed., *Susanna Wesley: The Complete Writings* (Oxford, New York, 1997), p. 9. It must also be acknowledged that Samuel did have a tendency to incur expenses that he could ill afford. For example, he had allowed himself to become the representative at the Diocese of Lincoln Convocation for a period of three years. This ruling body of the Church of England met for several months at a time in London, and each member covered his own expenses for travelling and accommodation – a cost of some £50 per year.

7 Clarke, *Memoirs of the Wesley Family*, vol. I, p. 192.

8 He described Lincoln Castle as 'the haven where I've long expected to be' (Letter, 25 June 1705).

9 Clarke, *Memoirs of the Wesley Family*, vol. I, p. 214.

10 Wallace, *Susanna Wesley: The Complete Writings*, p. 9.

11 Clarke, *Memoirs of the Wesley Family*, vol. I, p. 206.

12 Wallace, *Susanna Wesley: The Complete Writings*, p. 67.

13 Wallace, *Susanna Wesley: The Complete Writings*, p. 67.

14 Wallace, *Susanna Wesley: The Complete Writings*, p. 92.

15 Wallace, *Susanna Wesley: The Complete Writings*, p. 9.

16 A reference from Amos 4.11 and Zachariah 3.7.

17 Rattenbury, J. E., *Wesley's Legacy to the World* (London, 1928), p. 29.

18 Wallace, *Susanna Wesley: The Complete Writings*, p. 369.

19 Wallace, *Susanna Wesley: The Complete Writings*, p. 370.

20 It was the virtues of honesty, discipline, hard work and keeping promises that did so much to help working-class people into the new rising middle classes who were to occupy the pews in the Methodist chapels of the late eighteenth century and the whole of the nineteenth century.

21 *Letters*, 23 February 1724 or 1725.

22 Clarke, *Memoirs of the Wesley Family*, vol. II, p. 166.

23 Clarke, *Memoirs of the Wesley Family*, vol. I, p. 198.

24 Clarke, *Memoirs of the Wesley Family*, vol. I, p. 198.

25 Clarke, *Memoirs of the Wesley Family*, vol. I, p. 198.

26 Newton, John, *Susanna Wesley* (London, 1968), p. 39.

Chapter 3   Charterhouse and Christ Church

1 *Journal*, 28 June 1770.

2 Overton, J. H., *John Wesley* (London, 1905), p. 11.

3 Green, V. H. H., *Young Mr Wesley* (London, 1963), p. 66.

4 *Journal*, 24 May 1738.

5 *Letters*, 3 November 1721. It is difficult to assess the influence of Charterhouse on Wesley, but he certainly had an influence on Charterhouse. In 1919 the then headmaster, the Reverend Frank Fletcher, looking back over 200 years, said, 'We count John Wesley as the greatest of many Carthusians.' He is also the subject of a verse in the School Song.

6 Telford, J., ed., *The Letters of John Wesley*, 8 vols (London, 1931), vol. I, p. 5.

7 According to Telford, Wigan added to his pastoral duties the principalship of New Inn Hall, a hall of the university. In this second appointment it appears that he did not live up to expectations and attracted no new students to the Hall, which largely remained closed during his principalship.

8 Curnock, N., ed., *The Journal of John Wesley*, 8 vols (London, 1909), vol. I, p. 56.

9 Curnock, *Journal*, vol. I, p. 62.

10 *Letters*, 18 December 1724.

11 *Letters*, 23 September 1723.

12 *Letters*, 23 September 1723.

13 Green, *Young Mr Wesley*, p. 67.

14 *Journal*, 28 June 1770.

Chapter 4   Lincoln College and a Fellow's Life

1 Rack, Henry, *Reasonable Enthusiast: John Wesley and the Rise of Methodism* (London, 1989), p. 75.

2 Samuel was delighted by the news and in a letter to John implied that it somehow made up for all his own disappointments and debts (Tyerman, L., *The Life and Times of Samuel Wesley* (London, 1866), p. 399). Indeed, Samuel was so pleased with the outcome that he sent John £12 he could ill afford to part with (*Letters*, 4 April 1726). Following the election, John wrote to thank his brother for all the trouble he had taken to help him.

3 *Letters*, 4 April 1726.

4 Telford, John, ed., *The Letters of John Wesley*, 8 vols (London, 1931), vol. I, p. 26.

5 Green, V. H. H., *Young Mr Wesley* (London, 1963), p. 102.

6 Green, *Young Mr Wesley*, p. 120.

7 For a full account, see Baker, Frank, ed., *Works of John Wesley*, vol. 25 (Oxford, 1980), pp. 202–6.

8 Tyerman, L., *The Life and Times of the Revd John Wesley*, 3 vols (London, 1890), vol. I, p. 50.

9 *Letters*, 24 January 1727.

10 Tyerman, *John Wesley*, vol. I, p. 54.

11 Tyerman, *John Wesley*, vol. I, p. 81.

12 Schmidt, Martin, *John Wesley: A Theological Biography*, 2 vols (London, 1962, 1971, 1973), vol. I, p. 92.

13 Tyerman, *John Wesley*, vol. I, p. 55.

14 Wesley, John, *A Plain Account of Christian Perfection*, Epworth Press edition (London, 1970), p. 5.

15 Wesley, *A Plain Account of Christian Perfection*, p. 6.

16 Wesley, *A Plain Account of Christian Perfection*, p. 6.

17 *Letters*, John Wesley to his mother, 19 March 1727.

18 *Letters*, John Wesley to his mother, 28 February 1730.

19 Green, *Young Mr Wesley*, p. 100.

20 One of the people who belonged to his circle of acquaintances was Viscount Dupplin, son of the Seventh Earl of Kinnoull. On one occasion Wesley and Lord Dupplin met together with the Dean of Christ Church. Lord Kinnoull told the Dean of Christ Church that the greatest service the College could do for his son 'would be to prepare him to resist the influences of the ill examples he would see in the world' when he left College. On another occasion, Charles Wesley recorded in his Journal that he and John dined together with Lord Dupplin and his uncle, the Earl of Oxford. Shortly after his return to Oxford from the Christmas vacation, early in 1727, he met Dupplin for tea. It is also interesting to note that another member of the Kinnoull family became the Rector of Epworth and, unlike his immediate predecessor, permitted John Wesley to take Holy Communion in the parish church (Green, *Young Mr Wesley*, pp. 112, 113, 115).

21 Dr James Rigg, in his book *The Living Wesley* (London, 1891), p. 45, suggested that Wesley was infatuated with Betty, who later became Mrs Taylor, and he probably drew this conclusion because Sarah married the Reverend John Chapone, at Christmas 1725, soon after Wesley had come to know the family. Moreover, Rigg believed that a letter written by Robert Kirkham a year after Sarah's marriage indicated Robert's desire that Wesley would become his brother-in-law.

22 See Green, *Young Mr Wesley*, Rack, *Reasonable Enthusiast*, and Schmidt, *John Wesley*.

23 See Green, *Young Mr Wesley*, p. 199.

24 See Green, *Young Mr Wesley*, p. 201.

25 See Green, *Young Mr Wesley*, p. 199.

26 See Rack, *Reasonable Enthusiast*, p. 79.

27 See Rack, *Reasonable Enthusiast*, p. 78.

28 Telford, *Letters*, vol. I, p. 50.

29 *Letters*, to Mrs Pendarves, 12 September 1730 and 3 October 1730.

30 Schmidt, *John Wesley*, vol. I, p. 112.

31 *Letters*, from Mrs Pendarves, 15 January 1731.

32 *Letters*, to Mrs Pendarves, July 1734.

33 Schmidt, *John Wesley*, vol. I, p. 96.
34 *Letters*, to Richard Morgan, 18 October 1732.
35 *Letters*, to Richard Morgan, 18 October 1732.
36 *Letters*, to Richard Morgan, 18 October 1732.
37 Tyerman, *John Wesley*, vol. I, p. 83.
38 Rigg, James H., *The Living Wesley* (London, 1891), p. 73.
39 Green, *Young Mr Wesley*, p. 160.
40 Wesley's sermon, 'The Most Excellent Way'. Wesley, John, *Works*, 3rd edition, 14 vols (London, 1872), vol. VII, pp. 36–7.

Chapter 5 Georgia

 1 Tyerman, L., *The Life and Times of the Revd John Wesley*, 3 vols (London, 1890), vol. I, pp. 101–2; Green, V. H. H., *Young Mr Wesley* (London, 1963), p. 237.
 2 Lee, Umphrey, *The Lord's Horseman: John Wesley the Man* (London, 1956), p. 43.
 3 Overton, J. H., *John Wesley* (London, 1905), p. 45.
 4 Overton, *John Wesley*, p. 45.
 5 *Journal*, 14 October 1735.
 6 *Journal*, 25 January 1736.
 7 *Journal*, 25 January 1736.
 8 *Journal*, 2 December 1737.
 9 *Journal*, 24 February 1736.
10 *Journal*, 28 February 1736.
11 *Journal*, 27 July 1737.
12 See Watson, J. R., *The English Hymn* (Oxford, 1997), pp. 205–14.
13 Watson, *The English Hymn*, p. 206.
14 Schmidt, Martin, *John Wesley: A Theological Biography*, 2 vols (London, 1962, 1971, 1973), vol. I, p. 141.
15 *Journal*, 17 April 1735.
16 *Journal*, 5 May 1736.
17 For a full account of this event see Lee, *The Lord's Horseman*, pp. 47–9.
18 *Journal*, 22 June 1736.
19 *Journal*, 22 June 1736.
20 *Journal*, 25 January 1737.
21 *Diary*, 15 August 1736.
22 *Letters*, John Wesley to Charles Wesley, 22 March 1736.
23 Ethridge, William Snow, *Strange Fires* (New York, 1971), p. 193.
24 Ethridge, *Strange Fires*, p. 194.
25 In fairness to Wesley this may have arisen more from his desire that things should be done properly than from his sense of hurt. He did make the mistake of not at first sharing this thought with them, but talked to others

instead, with the result that Sophia and Williamson heard of his opinion through a third party, which naturally made them extremely angry.

26 Ethridge, *Strange Fires*, p. 214.
27 *Journal*, 11 August 1737.
28 Rigg, James H., *The Living Wesley* (London, 1891), p. 81.
29 Lee, *The Lord's Horseman*, p. 55.
30 Lee, *The Lord's Horseman*, p. 55.
31 Overton, *John Wesley*, p. 53.
32 Curnock, N., *The Journal of John Wesley*, 8 vols (London, 1909), vol. I, p. 426.
33 *Letters*, John Wesley to his brother Samuel, 23 November 1736.
34 *Journal*, 24 and 29 January 1738.
35 Overton, *John Wesley*, p. 58.
36 *Journal*, 3 February 1738.

Chapter 6   Failure and Conversion

1 Lee, Umphrey, *The Lord's Horseman: John Wesley the Man* (London, 1956), pp. 58–9.
2 *Letters*, John Wesley to his nephew, Samuel Wesley, 16 September 1789.
3 Rack, Henry, *Reasonable Enthusiast: John Wesley and the Rise of Methodism* (London, 1989), pp. 151ff, discusses this issue in some detail.
4 *Journal*, 4 March 1738.
5 *Journal*, 23 March 1738.
6 *Journal*, 22 April 1738.
7 *Letters*, letter from John Clayton to John Wesley, 1 May 1738.
8 *Journal*, 9 May 1738.
9 *Journal*, 10 May 1738.
10 *Journal*, 24 May 1738.
11 *Letters*, 30 October 1738.
12 *Journal*, 4 January 1739.
13 Rigg, James H., *The Living Wesley* (London, 1891), p. 122.
14 Sermon: 'The Catholic Spirit'. Henry Rack gives a detailed and helpful discussion of the evangelical versus the catholic element in Wesley's life; he also draws up an excellent summary of the divisions among scholars on the significance of Wesley's conversion. See Rack, *Reasonable Enthusiast*, pp. 145–7.

Chapter 7   Growth and Development

1 *Journal*, 1 May 1738.
2 *Letters*, to the Reverend Vincent Perronet, December 1748, later *A Plain Account of the People called Methodists*, London, 1749.
3 *Letters*, to the Reverend Vincent Perronet, December 1748.

4 Wesley, John, *Works*, 3rd edition, 14 vols (London, 1872), vol. VIII, p. 269.

5 Wesley, *Works*, vol. VIII, p. 262.

6 Vincent Perronet (1693–1785). For 39 years Perronet was Vicar of Shoreham in Kent. He supported and advised Wesley, and even reorganized his own parish on Wesley's principles, and two of his sons became lay preachers. Charles Wesley referred to Perronet as 'The Archbishop of Methodism'. The friendship between him and the Wesleys remained intact to the end of their lives.

7 Wesley, *Works*, vol. VIII, p. 253.

8 Wesley, *Works*, vol. VIII, p. 270.

Chapter 8   The Moravians and Stillness

1 *Journal*, 14 June 1738.

2 *Journal*, 10 August 1738.

3 *Letters*, letter from Philip Henry Molther to John Wesley, 25 January 1740.

4 *Journal*, 31 December 1739.

5 Rack, Henry, *Reasonable Enthusiast: John Wesley and the Rise of Methodism* (London 1989), p. 204.

6 *Journal*, 19 April 1740.

7 Southey, R., *Life of Wesley*, Cavendish edition (London, 1889), p. 183.

8 *Journal*, 5 June 1940.

9 *Journal*, 16 July 1740.

10 *Journal*, 23 July 1740.

11 Tyerman, L., *The Life and Times of the Revd John Wesley*, 3 vols (London, 1890), vol. I, pp. 300–1.

12 Southey, *Life of Wesley*, p. 186.

13 Rupp, Gordon, *Religion in England 1688–1791* (Oxford, 1986), p. 368.

Chapter 9   Wesley, Whitefield and Predestination

1 *Letters*, 13 February 1739.

2 *Letters*, George Whitefield to John Wesley, 25 June 1739.

3 *Letters*, George Whitefield to John Wesley, 2 July 1739.

4 *Letters*, George Whitefield to John Wesley, 23 July 1739.

5 Tyerman, L., *The Life and Times of the Revd John Wesley*, 3 vols (London, 1890), vol. I, p. 315.

6 Matthew 5.48.

7 *Letters*, George Whitefield to John Wesley, 26 March 1740.

8 *Letters*, George Whitefield to John Wesley, 25 September 1740.

9 *Letters*, George Whitefield to John Wesley, 26 March 1740.

10 *Letters*, John Wesley to George Whitefield, 9 August 1740.

11 *Journal*, 19 June 1740.

12 *Journal*, 19 June 1740.

13 *Journal*, 20 December 1740.

14 *Journal*, 22 February 1741.

15 *Journal*, 22 February 1741.

16 *Journal*, 6 March 1741.

17 Tyerman, *John Wesley*, vol. I, p. 344.

18 *Journal*, 28 March 1741.

19 *Letters*, to John Smith, 25 June 1746.

20 *Journal*, 24 August 1743.

21 *Letters*, 1 September 1748.

22 Wesley, John, *Works*, 3rd edition, 14 vols (London, 1872), vol.VI, p. 180.

Chapter 10   Preaching and the Preacher

1 Curnock, N., ed., *The Journal of John Wesley*, 8 vols (London, 1909), vol. III, p. 147.

2 Simon, J. S., *John Wesley and the Methodist Societies* (London, 1923), p. 56.

3 Tyerman, L., *The Life and Times of the Revd John Wesley*, 3 vols (London, 1890), vol. I, p. 449.

4 Wesley, John, *Forty-Four Sermons* (London, 1944), p. 42.

5 Wesley, *Forty-Four Sermons*, p. 48.

6 Wesley, *Forty-Four Sermons*, p. 46.

7 Tyerman, *John Wesley*, vol. I, p. 448.

8 *Journal*, 24 August 1744.

9 Simon, *John Wesley and the Methodist Societies*, p. 223.

10 *Journal*, 24 August 1744.

11 Graham Midgley, in his book *University Life in Eighteenth Century Oxford* (New Haven, 1996), vividly portrays some of these abuses.

12 Green, V. H. H., *Young Mr Wesley* (London, 1963), p. 144.

13 Tyerman, *John Wesley*, vol. I, p. 221.

14 *Journal*, vol. II, p. 156.

15 *Journal*, 31 March 1739.

16 *Journal*, 2 April 1739.

17 Lee, Umphrey, *The Lord's Horseman: John Wesley the Man* (London, 1956), p. 73.

18 *Journal*, 18 October 1749.

19 Rupp, Gordon, *Just Men* (London, 1977), p. 115.

20 Lee, *The Lord's Horseman*, p. 74.

21 Southey, R., *Life of Wesley* (London, 1889), p. 261.

22 Wood, A. Skevington, *The Burning Heart* (London, 1962), p. 140.

23 *Journal*, 5 May 1747.

24 Schmidt, Martin, *John Wesley: A Theological Biography*, 2 vols (London, 1962, 1971, 1973), vol. II, part 2, p. 9.

25 Rigg, James H., *The Living Wesley* (London, 1891), p. 131.

26 *Journal*, 14 June 1739.

27 *Journal*, 24 January 1743.

28 *Journal*, 30 September 1740.

29 *Journal*, 25 June 1745.

30 Southey, *Life of Wesley*, p. 256.

31 *Journal*, 31 October 1745.

32 Southey, *Life of Wesley*, p. 263.

33 Rigg, *The Living Wesley*, p. 130.

34 *Journal*, 1 May 1739.

35 *Journal*, 12 March 1743.

36 *Journal*, 26 June 1759, 6 September 1772.

37 *Journal*, 28 August 1748. Within ten years things must have greatly improved at St Paul's, for he noted on a visit to the cathedral that the congregation 'was very large and very attentive' (*Journal*, 10 March 1758).

38 Doughty, W. L., *John Wesley: Preacher* (London, 1955), p. 49.

39 Eliot, George, *Adam Bede,* World's Classics Edition (Oxford, 1996), p. 37.

Chapter 11   Opposition and Riots

1 Curnock, N., ed., *The Journal of John Wesley*, 8 vols (London, 1909), vol. II, p. 93.

2 Curnock, *Journal*, vol. II, p. 143.

3 Wesley, John, *A Plain Account of Christian Perfection* (London, 1952 edn), p. 15.

4 Wesley would have been aware of Canon 73, which placed restrictions on clergy meeting in private homes.

5 See Baker, Frank, *John Wesley and the Church of England* (London, 1970), p. 88.

6 John Wesley, *Works*, 3rd edition, 14 vols (London, 1872), vol. VIII, p. 214.

7 Wesley, *Works*, vol. VIII, p. 228.

8 Wesley, *Works*, vol. VIII, p. 492.

9 Wesley, *Works*, vol. VIII, p. 492.

10 Moore, Henry, *Life of the Rev. John Wesley*, 2 vols (London, 1824), vol. II, p. 415.

11 Wesley, *Works*, vol. VIII, p. 495.

12 Wesley, *Works*, vol. VIII, p. 495.

13 Overton, J. H., *John Wesley* (London, 1905), p. 58.

14 Rupp, Gordon, *Religion in England 1688–1791* (Oxford, 1986), p. 374.

15 Rupp, *Religion in England*, p. 178.

16 Lunn, Arnold, *John Wesley* (London, 1929), p. 224.

17 See *Journal*, 20 October 1743 for a full account.

18 *Journal*, 20 October 1743.
19 *Journal*, 4 July 1745.
20 *Journal*, 4 July 1745.
21 *Letters*, 26 August 1748.
22 *Journal*, 9 June 1742.

Chapter 12   The Travelling Preacher

1 *Journal*, 25 February 1765.
2 Wesley, John, *Works*, 3rd edition, 14 vols (London, 1872), vol. VIII, pp. 9–10.
3 Wesley, *An Earnest Appeal to Men of Reason and Religion*, in *Works*, vol. VIII, p. 8.
4 Wesley, *Works*, vol. VIII, p. 231.
5 *Journal*, 22 December 1765.
6 *Journal*, 21 March 1779.
7 *Journal*, 22 February 1745.
8 *Journal*, 23 February 1745.
9 *Journal*, 23 February 1745.
10 *Journal*, 22 October 1743.
11 *Journal*, 8–9 April 1764.
12 Wesley, *Works*, vol. XII, p. 242.
13 *Journal*, 27 July 1764.
14 Southey, R., *Life of Wesley* (London, 1889), p. 254.
15 *Journal*, 15 June 1770.
16 *Journal*, 30 May 1777.
17 *Journal*, 2 June 1777.
18 *Journal*, 2 June 1777.
19 *Journal*, 20 June 1774.
20 *Journal*, 13 August 1782.
21 *Journal*, 13 October 1790.
22 Wakeley, J. B., *Anecdotes of the Wesleys* (London, 1889), pp. 312–13.
23 Rupp, Gordon, *Just Men* (London, 1977), p. 127.
24 Lunn, Arnold, *John Wesley* (London, 1929), p. 256.
25 *Journal*, 13 October 1779.
26 *Journal*, 13 October 1779.
27 *Journal*, 18 July 1765.
28 *Journal*, 27 July 1764.
29 Doughty, W. L., *John Wesley: Preacher* (London, 1955), p. 196.
30 A similar comment is found in Curnock, N., ed., *The Journal of John Wesley*, 8 vols (London, 1909), vol. VII, p. 482.

Chapter 13   Theological and Matrimonial Strife

1 Wesley, John, *Forty-Four Sermons* (London, 1944), p. 450.
2 Lunn, Arnold, *John Wesley* (London, 1929), p. 267.
3 Leger, J. A., *John Wesley's Last Love* (London, 1910), p. 22.
4 Tyerman, L., *The Life and Times of the Revd John Wesley*, 3 vols (London, 1890), vol. II, p. 6.
5 Leger, *John Wesley's Last Love*, p. 1.
6 Leger, *John Wesley's Last Love*, p. 1.
7 Leger, *John Wesley's Last Love*, p. 2.
8 Lunn, *John Wesley*, p. 275.
9 *Journal*, vol. III, p. 435.
10 Tyerman, *John Wesley*, vol. II, p. 55.
11 Edwards, Maldwyn, *My Dear Sister* (Manchester, 1980), p. 39.
12 *Letters*, 2 April 1751.
13 *Letters*, 7 April 1751.
14 *Letters*, 27 March 1751.
15 *Journal*, 24 April 1752.
16 *Letters*, 22 May 1752.
17 *Letters*, 28 May 1757.
18 *Letters*, to Sarah Ryan, 27 January 1758.
19 *Letters*, vol. IV, p. 20.
20 *Letters*, 2 March 1759.
21 *Letters*, to his wife, 23 October 1759.
22 *Letters*, 12 July 1760.
23 *Letters*, 6 May 1766.
24 *Letters*, to Charles Wesley, 9 July 1766.
25 *Letters*, to Charles Wesley, 10 July 1772.
26 *Journal*, 30 June 1772.
27 *Letters*, 10 June 1774.
28 *Letters*, 18 May 1774.
29 Lunn, *John Wesley*, p. 295.
30 Tyerman, *John Wesley*, vol. III, p. 233.
31 Rigg, James H., *The Living Wesley* (London, 1891), p. 207.
32 *Letters*, 1 September 1777.
33 *Letters*, 2 October 1778.

Chapter 14   Social Concern

1 Williams, Basil, *The Whig Supremacy, 1714–1760* (Oxford, 1939), p. 125.
2 See Langford, Paul, *A Polite and Commercial People: England 1727–1783* (Oxford, 1989), chapter 4.

3 Rack, Henry, *Reasonable Enthusiast: John Wesley and the Rise of Methodism* (London, 1989), p. 360.

4 Wesley, John, *Forty-Four Sermons* (London, 1944), p. 579.

5 Wesley, John, *Works*, 3rd edition, 14 vols (London, 1872), vol. VI, pp. 127–8.

6 Wesley, *Works*, vol. VI, p. 133.

7 Wesley, *Works*, vol. VII, p. 9.

8 *Journal*, vol. VIII, p. 80.

9 *Journal*, 9 and 10 February 1753.

10 *Journal*, 21 March 1753.

11 *Journal*, 21 January 1740.

12 *Journal*, 7 May 1741.

13 *Journal*, 24 February 1747.

14 Bebb, E. D., *Wesley: A Man with A Concern* (London, 1960), p. 107.

15 *Journal*, 7 May 1741.

16 *Journal*, 5 December 1785.

17 *Letters*, to Vincent Perronet, December 1748.

18 *Journal*, 14 March 1790.

19 *Letters*, to Vincent Perronet, December 1748.

20 *Journal*, 20 November 1767.

21 Rack, *Reasonable Enthusiast*, p. 444.

22 *Journal*, 3 February 1753.

23 *Journal*, 16 October 1760.

24 *Journal*, 16 October 1760.

25 *Journal*, 28 July 1787.

26 *Journal*, 15 March 1782.

27 *Journal*, 23 March 1749.

28 *Journal*, 22 November 1756.

29 *Journal*, 6 December 1756.

30 For a wider discussion of this topic see the unpublished papers of Donald Tranter (to be found in the Library, Harris Manchester College, Oxford), who wrote authoritatively and extensively on Wesley and education.

31 *Letters*, 12 October 1778.

32 See Tranter, Donald, MS, 'John Wesley and the Education of Children', 1995.

33 Tranter, 'John Wesley and the Education of Children'.

34 Wesley, John, *A Plain Account of Kingswood School* (1781) in Wesley, *Works*, vol. XIII, p. 296.

35 *Journal*, 21 June 1751.

36 Tranter, 'John Wesley and the Education of Children'.

37 *Journal*, 29 September–15 October 1750.

38 Tranter, 'John Wesley and the Education of Children'.

39 *Letters*, 25 March 1747.

40 *Letters*, to Vincent Perronet, December 1748.

41 *Journal*, 4 December 1746.

42 *Letters*, to Vincent Perronet, December 1748.

43 *Letters*, to John Smith, 25 March 1747.

44 *Letters*, to John Smith, 25 March 1747.

45 In the 1780 edition, as Wesley kept adding new cures to subsequent editions.

46 Hill, A. Wesley, *John Wesley Among the Physicians* (London, 1958), p. 125.

47 *Journal*, 9 November 1756.

48 Hill, *John Wesley Among the Physicians*, p. 92.

49 *Letters*, to Mr Hawes, 20 July 1776.

50 Hill, *John Wesley Among the Physicians*, p. 32.

51 *The Medical Officer*, October 1956.

52 *Journal*, 12 February 1772.

53 Wesley, *Works*, vol. XI, pp. 59–79.

54 Wesley, *Works*, vol. XI, p. 69.

55 Wesley, *Works*, vol. XI, p. 79.

56 Wesley, *Works*, vol. XIII, p. 153.

57 Wesley, *Works*, vol. XII, p. 507.

58 *Journal*, 4 March 1788.

59 Wesley, *Works*, vol. XIII, p. 153.

Chapter 15   Farewell

1 Curnock, N., ed., *The Journal of John Wesley*, 8 vols (London, 1909), vol. VII, p. 173.

2 *Journal*, 28 June 1786.

3 *Journal*, 1 March 1788.

4 Watson, Richard, *John Wesley* (London, 1831), p. 160.

5 Wesley's text for his beloved follower was: 'Mark the perfect man, and behold the upright, for the end of that man is peace.'

6 Tyerman, L., *The Life and Times of the Revd John Wesley*, 3 vols (London, 1890), vol. III, p. 427.

7 Tyerman, *John Wesley*, vol. III, p. 428.

8 *Journal*, 20 January 1746.

9 *Letters*, 10 September 1784.

10 *Letters*, 20 September 1788.

11 Tyson, John, *Charles Wesley* (Oxford, 1989), p. 437.

12 Gill, F., *Charles Wesley* (London, 1964), p. 222.

13 *Letters*, 18 February 1788.

14 Tyson, *Charles Wesley*, p. 480.

15 Tyerman, *John Wesley*, vol. III, p. 527.

16 *Journal*, 3 September 1788.

17 *Journal*, 15 December 1788.

18 *Journal*, 1 January 1789.
19 *Letters*, 24 November 1787; and Tyerman, *John Wesley*, vol. III, p. 501.
20 *Journal*, 3 June 1790.
21 *Journal*, 5 April 1790.
22 *Journal*, 30 November 1789.
23 *Letters*, 26 June 1790.
24 *Letters*, 1 February 1791.
25 *Journal*, 4 July 1790.
26 *Letters*, 27 June 1766.
27 Thompson, E. P., *The Making of the English Working Class* (Harmondsworth, 1968), p. 389.
28 Rattenbury, J. E., *Wesley's Legacy to the World* (London, 1928), p. 229.
29 See Thompson, *The Making of the English Working Class*.

Author's note

There are several editions of John Wesley's *Journal* and of his *Letters,* so that when referring to them I have invariably given the dates of the letters and of the entries in the *Journal,* rather than a specific edition and page number. References therefore can be found regardless of the edition available.

Index